Born To Be Happy

How to Uncover Your Natural State
of Happiness

Alex P. Keats

Right Now
Publishing

Right Now Publishing

ISBN-13:978-0615929132

ISBN-10:0615929133

First Printing, 2012

Printed in the United States of America

Other books by Alex P. Keats::

When Wisdom Blooms: Awaken The Sage
Within

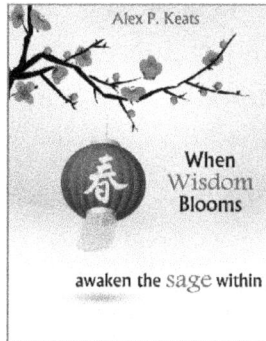

When we're born, we didn't come with an operating manual showing us how to live from our natural state of wisdom. All the parts were in the box, but the directions were left out. And since most around us still haven't cracked the code, it's no wonder why we experience so many challenges in life. And yet if wisdom really is fully present and available within each one of us, why does it seem so difficult to access and live from? Wisdom is the power to see what is always and already right and true. It's that aspect of ourselves that innately possesses the ability to discern truth from falsehood.

If wisdom is a flower that only blossoms under the proper conditions, we are wise to know what those conditions are. Conversely, we are wise to notice what suppresses our innate wisdom so that it's opposite quality, ignorance, doesn't blossom. Wouldn't the quality of our lives then, ultimately be dependent upon which half blooms? What might happen if we put aside everything we've accumulated up to this point, and suspend all that we think we know for a time, for the very real possibility of experiencing a different reality, right now? Well, let's find out.

The Dance of Imperfection: Living in Perfect Harmony with Life

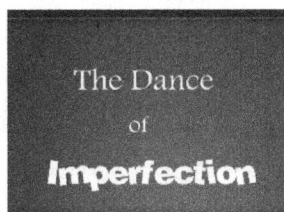

The Dance
of
Imperfection

Living in
Perfect Harmony
with Life

Alex P. Keats

Conventional wisdom would have us believe perception is reality, and that if we believe a thing about ourselves, it must be true. However, for anything to exist, for anything to be real, it must be present and observable. In other words, we must have the ability to validate its existence in our experience – and not just simply in our minds. Just because we perceive something to be real, doesn't mean it's real, does it? The fact is we give all kinds of false concepts existence – and we suffer. The antidote is simple and profound, and it takes literally no effort on our part.

The solution is to question whether there is, or has ever been such a thing as "defects" in our character, or "flaws" in our makeup. What tells us this? Can we absolutely know this is true? Aside from in our perceptual interpretations, where is it? If we can't find it upon the closest examination, why do we insist on giving life to something that has no existence in reality, *especially* if it hurts? Once the idea of imperfection was believed in, we've spent so much time and energy towards compensating for, and running from our self-perceptions we assume to be real.

We've wasted so much energy entertaining and believing in the mind's assertions like, "I'm not good enough," "Others have it, but I don't," and "If only I could get rid of my faults, then I'd be happy and secure," instead of examining their reality in the first place. Like a house of cards, it all collapses when the plug is pulled on the notion that there's actually a valid reason to feel insecure and unworthy! It all collapses when we root out and sever the main belief that says, "Imperfection is a fact of existence we all have to cope with!"

Only when we re-examine what we've been told, and only when we investigate and see it's not just a matter of semantics, will we allow ourselves to authentically embrace all of who we are. No longer do we engage in mind strategies that continue to reinforce the basic error. Free from the need to compensate for, or distract ourselves from our once-perceived imperfections, the desire to bolster or cultivate *anything* drops away. We simply enjoy life, living spontaneously from being – in perfect harmony with life.

Dedication

This book is dedicated to my wonderful and loving parents, Joe and Kay, who possessed an extraordinary amount of patience and compassion when it came to dealing with all the years of unhappiness I couldn't help but spread around.

Happiness arises spontaneously for the one who sees how experience unfolds.

Contents

Introduction

Sadly, most people live their lives – all the way to the grave – not being truly happy. What's even more unfortunate is that it doesn't have to be this way.

What's unfortunate is that we don't have to go through our lives experiencing so little joy, while clinging to the fleeting moments of feeling happy.

It's a natural human impulse to want to experience true and lasting happiness. It's only natural to want to experience as much happiness as we can, isn't it?

Don't you sense that?

When you're happy, don't you have a tendency to want to share it with others? Of course you do. Happiness is a vibration – like everything else – and it's contagious!

You may have heard countless times that "happiness is a choice" and that you can choose it in any moment.

IF being happy is simply a matter of choice, then why would you ever choose to be unhappy?

Why would you ever choose unhappiness when you can choose happiness?

If happiness is indeed a choice, isn't it very strange then, that so many people wake up each day choosing to be unhappy? It doesn't make a whole lot of sense, does it?

While there is some bit of truth in the statement that happiness is a choice, there's so much more to the formula of being happy.

Most books on happiness claim that in order to be happy, you must engage in certain types of behaviors and refrain from others. In other words, "choose" the behaviors that bring happiness and refrain from those that don't.

While there is also some bit of truth in this, there's so much more to the formula of being happy.

Have you noticed that your actual and direct experience of this popular approach is usually very short-lived, having a beginning, middle and an end ... like all experience?

In other words, the happiness you feel (as a result of this approach) is a fleeting experience and not something that is organically present most of the time.

It's a manufactured happiness that comes and goes – and not the happiness that sticks around for the long haul. Techniques and methods for happiness by nature can't last.

That said, I don't mean to imply that it's a useless approach, nor am I criticizing all those well-intended authors. After all, there IS a direct relationship between happiness and how we behave, right?

What I am saying is that there's a fundamental flaw in this type of approach. Since most of it isn't based in timeless truths, it must fail to deliver the lasting happiness we desire.

So here's the invitation: Instead of using an "either or" approach to happiness, let's use a "both and" orientation and notice the difference in our long-term experience.

If being happy was a game, like any other game, there must be rules. Without rules, the game wouldn't make much sense. And like any game, who plays to lose?

This book is about discovering what those rules ARE and then abiding by those rules.

This book is about working with – and not against those rules – in order to win the game.

Can I assume you want to win? I mean, really win?

There are no "secrets" to happiness and there never was. All those authors out there telling you that there are "hidden secrets" to anything (including happiness) are flat out lying to you.

In fact, they are manipulating you, manipulating your desires and emotions in order to fatten their wallets because they are acutely aware that one of the greatest human motivators is the fear of loss.

They know that if they can convince you that there are secrets that you don't presently know about, secrets that would give you what you desperately want, that you'll purchase what they are selling – or you'll lose out!

If you do a search on how many self-help books (or DVDs or other materials) have the word "secrets" in their titles, you'll see what I mean.

It's natural to be drawn to these sorts of titles because they seem to imply there's something you don't know, something that's been withheld from you.

It's a common marketing trick, to be honest, and it irks me to no end.

Think about the last time you bought a product of some sort that promised a transformation of sorts based on some type of "secret."

Didn't you feel an energetic longing and a natural curiosity that led you to pull out your credit card, sometimes so fast that you hadn't even finished reading the product description?

I fell for this so many times and was always disappointed when the so-called "secrets" didn't work ... or at the very least, were not the magical solution they were presented to be.

Do that enough times, as I did, and it can really take the wind out of your sails.

Here's what I know: Your own inner wisdom doesn't need manipulation. There is no magic. There are no secrets.

But (and this is hugely critical) if you don't know how to uncover the "happiness wisdom" that already resides within you, then they might as well be secrets because the truth is, the wisdom lies untapped within you, like a forgotten treasure buried underneath the very foundation of your house.

As you read this book, you'll discover how to find that treasure already within you. More importantly, you'll discover how to open that treasure. You'll see that it's been sitting there all along and you'll jump for joy when you uncover it.

It's actually simple – and since our minds love to complicate things – we sometimes make it harder on ourselves than we really have to.

Wouldn't you agree that the most profound truths in life are often the simplest ones?

Don't fall into the trap of thinking you need to undertake a complicated journey to "seek" happiness.

In fact, because we are essentially no different, I am convinced that this book is all you'll need to uncover the happiness that is your natural state.

No, I'm not exaggerating.

In chapter 3, you'll discover the one thing that you absolutely must do in order to be genuinely happy almost all the time. I say "almost all the time" because in life, pain is inevitable.

It's what we do with the pain that makes all the difference.

It's my sincerest hope that you'll experience many "A-HA!" moments while reading these pages, moments that can ultimately deliver the real happiness you seek – IF you play by the rules.

It's time to tell you one very crucial thing: Throughout the course of this book you'll come across the phrase, "don't believe me, find out for yourself."

The reason I repeat this so often is because I am acutely aware that it is human nature to rely on belief instead of checking in with our own direct experience and see what our bodies are telling us.

There IS a way to find out what's true and what isn't. Sometimes we don't know, can't know – but the key is NOT to draw a conclusion that creates a belief.

Be willing to not know; it's another rule in this game of happiness.

This "don't believe me, find out for yourself" phrase isn't meant to annoy you or insult your intelligence.

It's simply a friendly reminder to point you back to your own experience – without relying on belief, without creating belief.

We often ignore what are bodies are telling us. There's so much wisdom in the body and it speaks to us moment to moment.

The question is, do we listen? Do we listen when our bodies are contracting and not at ease – and see why? Do we listen when our bodies are relaxed and at peace – and trace it back and see why?

You may wonder why I am qualified to even write a book on the subject – or even if I am. I don't blame you one bit. I'd wonder the same thing.

Who wants to read a book by an author who doesn't walk their talk? I sure wouldn't want to.

Happiness was something that escaped me for a good chunk of my adult life.

Granted, I was pretty happy as a kid and my parents truly loved me, but at the age of about sixteen or seventeen, things started to really change.

Without going into my full story here (you'll read more of it in chapters 10 through 12), I was the type of person who would openly share with you just how unhappy I was.

It was as if I was walking around and pointing to my open wounds and saying, "See, look here, it really hurts."

I can only imagine what a joy I was to be around and I wonder how many people would duck around the corner when they saw me coming.

I can honestly tell you that these days, I travel light. It is my sincere intention to show YOU how to do the same, that is, if you want it enough.

And since it's contagious, naturally I want to share it with you.

But enough of my story, this is about YOU.

I don't like to throw guarantees around, mostly because they're basically for the mind that needs to know in order to feel safe and secure in this world.

Besides, the truth is, tomorrow isn't guaranteed. The truth is, your next breath isn't even guaranteed, either.

Since it's very likely you will be gifted with a next breath and you will be gifted with another tomorrow, I will give you a very solid and absolute guarantee:

Uncovering your natural state of happiness won't happen a moment sooner than it's meant to happen.

Knowing this truth, you can relax.

Truth and relaxation go hand in hand.

When we see and realize what's true, something lets go.

What's MOST important is that you are earnest and rigorously honest with yourself – and willing to see for yourself what's true and what isn't true in your actual experience.

The above statement is so critically significant that I really must ask you to read it one more time. Will you? Good.

This "game of happiness" really isn't that difficult a game to play IF you're willing to really LOOK and SEE what its rules are and how it's played in order to win.

I can tell you that unconsciously relying on belief and assumptions isn't one of the rules!

Here's another rule: Always be mindful that the word is never the thing. The concept is never the actual.

Can you drink the word "water?"

Can you be burned by the word "fire?"

No, of course you can't.

Any word (concept) or group of words you ever read anywhere is never the thing. It's never the actual. They are "pointers" to the actual, not the actual itself.

Consequently, we see that language and descriptions aren't the reality, either ... and can only point to the actual.

This book is no different. However, this book is full of pointers to the real – pointers that (IF investigated and tested out in your own experience) can uncover what you already know to be true.

If you're presently aware of a belief that tells you that you don't deserve to be happy – or that it's only reserved for others, bring that along with you.

All is welcome here.

In fact, absolutely nothing will be left out and you'll soon see that you are all of it and that there is no escape from anything you feel or perceive.

See the truth in the wisdom of no escape.

To resist any part of it is to bring more of what you don't want. Once you really SEE this, you're playing in a whole different ballpark.

In Chapter 5, you'll recognize (and remember) something that is absolutely critical as you look to uncover your natural state of happiness.

Once you see this and prove it true for yourself, not only are you playing in a different ballpark, now you're playing in a ballpark with the clearest and brightest, illuminating lights.

Once you discover how it all works and consciously live in alignment with your natural state of happiness, it begins to take on a life of its own.

You'll find, much to your delight, that living in harmony with your natural state of happiness unfolds automatically and spontaneously by itself – but ONLY AFTER you see what's really true.

I can't tell you how cool this is.

I can tell you this without a shred of doubt: you already possess the blueprint within you right now – and that you need nothing other than a sincere and nonjudgmental willingness to look and see for yourself.

This book is the blueprint that will show you where to look so that you can confirm it experientially for yourself and validate what you already know.

Don't ever believe a word you read here and don't believe what others say.

That's a rule.

Find out for yourself.

This book will show you how to read (and apply) that blueprint in your own life so that you can uncover and uncover your natural state of happiness.

Here's a disclaimer: You won't "learn" a thing here because that implies you don't already know.

You will, however, recognize and uncover what you've always known but have simply forgotten.

And then you'll pass it on (because that's what we do) and your presence will bring comfort and ease to those around you. In fact, you may even be a joy to those around you.

Please know that I'm NOT assuming that you're presently miserable and unhappy. How can I know this?

I'd be pretty foolish to believe just because you're reading this that you're absolutely miserable and unhappy, wouldn't I?

Perhaps you want more happiness or maybe you want to find out why you aren't as happy as you'd like to be?

You may be curious to see if this book might tell you anything different than others you've read before on the subject.

You may even be curious to see if there might be one golden nugget here that opens you up in a way that you've never experienced before.

You may even be as happy as you want to be and just want to read how this author points to the happiness that already is your natural state.

Either way, it doesn't matter. There are no coincidences and besides, your reasons aren't critical.

IF you actually experiment and really see for yourself and IF you approach the words you are about to read as if it's the first time you've ever read a book on happiness, then something very beautiful can happen for you – yes, you.

IF you literally drop all your concepts, beliefs and conclusions about what you think it takes to be truly happy – and commit to not believing a word you read here – you're playing by the rules.

IF you follow along and experiment with these simple yet powerful pointers, your natural state of happiness will reveal itself in ways you never imagined – and in circumstances and situations you never imagined.

Once you discover how you've been blocking it, happiness will naturally arise in situations that will surprise and delight you.

So, for the time and energy you invest in reading this book, I humbly ask two things of you. First, consider the possibility that I really am pointing you in the right direction, okay?

Secondly, I ask that you absorb this book slowly and find out for yourself what's really true in your experience without relying on belief, okay?

Can you do this? Can you come from this place? If you can, you're much more likely to uncover your natural state of happiness.

Obviously, you're free to read this book in any way you like, but if you want the most benefit, I do highly recommend this way.

So discard anything that you think you know to be true about happiness, no matter what. Leave all that stuff at the door because it won't be needed here.

Because you ARE worth it, you may even want to take your shoes off before you enter – and bring a spirit of reverence and innocence to this undertaking.

All that's needed here is your willingness to follow through and go beyond conceptual belief and see if the following statement is ultimately true in your experience:

You need nothing to be happy; you need something to be sad.

Together, let us prove this by exploring experientially and not conceptually for it is only when we experience a thing in our being that true knowing occurs.

In the beginning of the sixteenth century, Michelangelo was asked how he was able to create the masterpiece Statue of David in such remarkably, fine detail. He said this:

"In every block of marble I see a statue as plain as though it stood before me, shaped and perfect in attitude and action. I have only to hew away the rough walls that imprison the lovely apparition to reveal it to the other eyes as mine see it."

Uncovering your natural state of happiness requires a very similar vision and attitude as the one Michelangelo possessed.

So get out your tools of focus, attention and awareness. Don't forget to bring willingness, wonder, great curiosity and courage, too.

Like Michelangelo, prepare yourself to chip away all that covers up your natural state of happiness – and watch what eventually must reveal itself.

Don't be surprised when you see that (all along) it was all so very simple – and that it was your mind that insisted it was complex.

Don't be surprised when you see that there never was such a thing as a true belief.

And you believed it.

It gives me great joy to share this direct "no secrets, nothing held back" book with you.

I'd be honored if you decide to investigate this seemingly elusive thing called happiness with me.

It may very well end up being the most fulfilling and rewarding thing you've ever done.

A Note To The Reader

I welcome you to these pages you're about to read – or perhaps I should I say, that you're about to immerse yourself in.

Have you ever read a book in which you felt it was just you and the author, perhaps alone in a room, intimately engaged in a timely conversation about the things most significant to you, things that normally wouldn't come up in your everyday life with those you associate with?

It is my wish for *that* sense to arise within you – where it's just you and me, alone together in a completely safe environment, intent on looking at what may prevent happiness from spontaneously arising in your experience – and just as important, to rediscover the various ways in which true happiness *does* arise.

Haven't you always suspected that real and lasting happiness is for you, too … and not just reserved for the lucky or the fortunate?

And haven't you also suspected the distinct possibility that there might be *something* in your consciousness that's keeping you from enjoying life to the fullest?

Either way, I have complete and absolute trust that your inner wisdom (that we all possess) knows what's real and true, despite what your mind thinks. By looking and identifying what your mind *believes* to be true and real, you take the first crucial step in uncovering your natural state of happiness.

Please be advised that you'll get so much more out of this book if you read it from below the neck – where your heart wisdom resides – and not with an analytical, comparative mind that likes to evaluate and judge what it reads with what it *thinks or believes it knows* from past experience.

Read this book and drink deeply from the experience that exists BEHIND and BEYOND the mere words. And find that experience within yourself as you go about your day after you put this book down.

This is something to be lived from your innermost self rather than from an act of simple reading comprehension – or as an act of just reading "about" concepts.

I hope that makes sense because it's so vitally important. There will be times throughout this book where you'll read a sentence and want to put the book down because it struck such a personal and profound chord within you.

I encourage you to listen to that pause and to live within that pause ... and to keep looking in the direction where you're being pointed ... because the word or concept is never the actual.

It's just not possible to stress how important this is. If you truly DO desire lasting happiness (that *isn't* dependent on circumstance or condition) it takes a sincere willingness to explore and test these concepts.

By "explore" I mean *experientially* and not just *thinking* about them.

If indeed it is our perspective that really does determine our experience, it stands to reason that *this* kind of orientation can only greatly increase the possibility where stable, permanent and transformational shifts happen – shifts that bring about what you've sensed and desired all along.

There's one last very significant thing worth mentioning. You'll come across the word "see" many times throughout this book. The way it's intended is not to "see" with your physical eyes, but rather, with your nonphysical, conscious awareness.

For example: *See* what's true. When we *see* what's true, we *realize* what's true – not in our heads but in our hearts, in our gut.

So go right ahead, my friend, dive in. I eagerly await your full and present participation in our uncommon dialogue.

If after reading this book you want to explore further, upcoming books called *When Wisdom Blooms: Awaken the Sage Within* and *The Dance of Imperfection: Living in Perfect Harmony with Life* will be coming out in the middle of August 2012. Until then, enjoy yourself and keep it real.

~ Alex P. Keats, March 2012

Chapter 1
You've Been Conditioned To Be Unhappy

People have been unhappy since time began, losing their jobs, their homes, their spouse, their children and even their lives but that's life, is it not?

We do our best to deal with it, don't we? Much of this capacity to cope is predicated on what we're presently aware of in that moment in time, based on our perspective and our past experiences.

We possess remarkable instincts and unmatched intellectual capacity – and the ingenuity to transform innovative ideas into reality.

When it comes to negotiating our emotional lives, however, we have a tendency to contract and go into an unconscious, trance-like state – a state that typically ends up not being real effective, at least not towards experiencing what we truly want.

We have a tendency to want to crawl in bed, pull up the covers and disappear, until it dawns on us that life must go on.

Instead of asking why these things happen or wondering what kind of God would allow these things to happen, we rarely see that there must be something we have to discover here – that there must be something to see here.

Instead of offering ourselves to the glory and beauty that is life, we lose ourselves in thinking. We lose ourselves in thinking about what should or could be happening instead of dealing with reality – or what is actually happening.

And since we also have a tendency to believe what our minds are telling us, we suffer.

We engage in the fantasy of the past and the fantasy of the future, while neither have any reality. We keep the past alive with memory and anticipate the future with our imagination.

But then a very interesting thing happens. When we're threatened with our very existence, when we're told that we only have two or three weeks to live, suddenly we realize that life is so precious.

All of a sudden, we become aware of our next breath, the sound of the wind blowing in the trees, the birds singing and all the wondrous diversity on display all around us.

Deep gratitude, a sense of wonder and awe – and a burning desire to live become our experience and we take nothing for granted anymore. Oh, how much we want to live!

Very few of us speak of now or attend to now – yet everyone craves to be now – whether we are conscious of this or not.

This is what we're all endeavoring to do, to bring our minds to rest by consciously living in this present moment only, where problems don't exist, where happiness does exist, whether we know it or not.

To live in the reality where there's no past or future is to live in the kingdom of heaven. When we realize that the kingdom of heaven is within us, then it must happen outside of us.

This is a law of life.

When we experientially realize that the kingdom of heaven is within us – when we see that the present moment is THE reality – then our natural state of happiness shines through, radiating in all directions.

When we don't, we identify with the thinking mind. We believe what our minds tell us. In fact, we believe most of what our minds tell us – even if it makes us miserable.

We seldom ever look at the cause of all of our stress and strain – and we cling to our beliefs, opinions and preferences (like sticky Velcro) as if our lives depended on them – as well as our religions, dogmas and theories.

We don't always see that all of this causes inner division that not only must be felt and experienced by us, but by those around us, too.

And ironically, none of what we cling to brings us what we want, yet we continue on, usually in the same fashion, not realizing that the happiness we seek is right here and right now … waiting patiently for us to see it needs nothing to shine.

In fact, it's already shining, like the sun above the nastiest stormy weather you could imagine. Your natural state of happiness is like the sun, self-shining in all directions, untouched and unharmed.

So why is this all so difficult and foreign to most of us? Why isn't happiness our actual experience most of the time, especially since mankind is so much more advanced now?

For starters, we were rarely ever shown this – and we rarely ever witnessed this "happiness for no special reason" in those around us.

Like a pot of clay molded by a potter at his wheel, we've been conditioned to be happy (only when specific circumstances and conditions are met) and we've been conditioned to believe happiness is a result of when "good things" happen to us.

On the face of things, I agree that this seems ludicrous, but sadly it is true. Let's explore this notion that we've been condition-ed to be unhappy further, shall we?

Granted, in the first 6-12 months, babies are happy just as long as their basic needs are met, but then something else starts to happen.

They gradually learn to be unhappy because they're taught to be unhappy.

And it's unintentional. I mean, who decides to have a baby with the intent of raising an unhappy child?

Weren't you rewarded early on for the behaviors your parents (or guardian) approved of and punished for the behaviors they disapproved of?

How many times did you hear the words, "bad boy" or "bad girl" when you behaved in ways they didn't like?

Consequently, you (unconsciously) linked up your behaviors with your self worth and this in turn affected your degree of happiness ... because it had to.

You were a small child, how could you know any better?

How many of us were actually taught that we weren't our behaviors? How many of us were taught that our inherent self worth is untouched and unharmed by our actions and behaviors – that is has absolutely nothing to do with our actions and behaviors?

I'd say less than one percent of us.

Every time you were scolded and heard "no, don't do that!" another layer was added onto your natural state of happiness.

You've most likely been taught (since you were a toddler) that happiness is reserved for those that do what's expected of them.

You were taught (more often with subtle messages) that those who attained the things in life that others deemed most worthwhile were the happiest – and those that earned the respect and admiration of others were the happiest.

Even if you didn't receive a lot of this conditioning at home, wouldn't it be accurate to say that most of us were raised in a culture where we learned that in order to be truly happy, we must have the right education and a good paying job?

How about a nice car and wardrobe ... a nice home and plenty of money in the bank, too?

Today it's much more overt. Just turn on the television, open the newspaper, check your smart phone and read the magazines. It's certainly all over the Internet, isn't it?

Today's generation is constantly bombarded with this message.

Since profit is such a driving force in this world, much of it is marketing and the attempt to get you to purchase something, but haven't we come to believe that what they're pitching equals happiness? Isn't that what the sly marketers want?

Hasn't this message actually become a living, organic thing within us? Hasn't it become so ingrained in our collective consciousness – or should I say collective unconsciousness – that we believe it and act on it?

No wonder that real and lasting happiness is the exception and not the rule for so many of us! None of this was or is true, but we believed it … and so our lives went, so our life goes.

While it can seem to make a whole lot of sense to go to battle with our conditioning, pointing the finger and playing the blame game only makes it worse and locks it into our experience.

For many years, I beat myself up over so many things. No wonder I was depressed and living a life of quiet desperation. Nonetheless, I always knew there was a way out.

Beating yourself up can only give your conditioning more power over you. More important, beating yourself up is a result of ignorance – and happens when we think we are to "blame" for our unhappiness. This attitude, this perspective, allows your conditioning to remain in the driver's seat, with its hands gripped firmly on the steering wheel, taking YOU for a ride.

While we aren't to blame for our unhappiness, we are responsible for our happiness.

Again, nobody (including ourselves) intentionally wanted us to be unhappy, at least not those that truly loved and cared for us.

You've forgotten that happiness is your natural state because everyone else around you – including your parents, siblings, friends and teachers has forgotten it. Even your mentors and therapists have forgotten it. They too, must live out what they believe.

It's been forgotten (or buried over if you prefer) due to a lifetime of countless untruths piled on top of each other, one belief, one assumption and one opinion at a time.

This is neither wrong or right, it just is. Generations of this conditioning occurred – and will continue to occur, until it doesn't anymore, until our consciousness is raised.

Consciousness is a funny thing. It's easily influenced and it easily succumbs to hypnotic, trance-like states, states where we walk around numb wondering why the heck we aren't that happy.

Unless you make happiness a top priority in your life – and act in accord with this priority – and unless you really look at what's suppressing your natural state of happiness, not much will change.

As the saying goes, if nothing changes, nothing changes.

Take five minutes right now and write down some examples that you recall from your own childhood. What sorts of things were you told that might have taught you that your worth was based on how you behaved or what you achieved?

How did that shape the person you are today? What would it feel like to not have anything to "live up to"?

Will you break the chain? Will you stand up and say enough is enough?

Will you commit to discovering why it is that happiness is such an elusive thing for so many, perhaps even for you?

I sincerely hope so because if you do, you can be a shining example for so many – and you can have such an impact on this world that needs you.

Happiness is truly a contagion that this world needs to catch!

This world is suffering from a severe lack of happiness and it all starts with you uncovering this "open secret" to being happy.

The fact that you are here reading these words is a very good sign, don't you agree?

The best way not to experience happiness is to go searching for it.

How's that for a paradox?

Instead, seek not happiness … instead seek (look at) what suppresses happiness and watch happiness reveal itself.

Like Michelangelo, chip away all that is untrue and watch happiness reveal itself in ways you never could imagine.

Chapter 2
The Hole That Can Never Be Filled

Unless you decide to go live in a cave in the Himalayas, a Zen monastery or a shack in the woods with no television or Internet, it's unlikely you'll escape this constant message that in order to be truly happy, certain conditions must be met.

If one believes that something more is needed for happiness – and that something better or different is needed for happiness – more money, more sex, more power or more recognition, then that individual will inevitably experience lack and limitation.

So what to do? Is there an escape or way out here? How do we fill the hole inside, that hole that tells us that we are incomplete unless we achieve that certain thing, be in a certain type of relationship or gain the respect and admiration of those we deem important?

Can there ever be a point where we've accumulated enough stuff to make us happy?

Have you concluded that real happiness is for others and not you?

Or might it be possible that we're asking the wrong questions? Is it possible that we're looking in the wrong direction when it comes to our own happiness?

If we want to enjoy a spectacular sunset, will we have that ability if we're facing east? No, of course not.

We must turn completely around (180 degrees) and face the right direction if we want to experience that sunset.

Have you ever considered that maybe the better questions are, "In what ways am I suppressing my natural state of happiness?

Another great question we might ask is, "Is the conditioning I received even true – and based in reality?"

Do you see how these kinds of questions determine your orientation and therefore, your experience?

Do you have a belief that you really need the approval of others to be happy and content?

If so, what tells you so?

How might your experience be different if you knew without any doubt at all – because you are totally secure with yourself – that what others think of you is none of your business?

Probably very liberating, wouldn't you say?

Is it really about achieving the goals we set for ourselves that is the key to this thing called happiness? Is it really about satisfying every desire we have that brings lasting happiness?

Face the proper direction and contemplate the truth (whether you realize it or not right now) that you literally don't need anything to be happy!

How do we rid ourselves of this void inside that never seems to go away? Is this void even real, despite it feeling real?

For starters, stop believing the voice that says "you need so and so" in order to be happy.

Just because these thoughts arise in your mind, does it mean they're true?

Does it?

Ask yourself, "How do I know this is really true?" Ask yourself, "How can I know this is true?"

Please don't skip over these questions because the answers you arrive at just may radically change your life.

Would you agree that you don't know what you don't know?

That you're unaware of what you aren't aware of? I just sensed that you just nodded your head yes … so let's continue with this theme.

Admittedly, this seems very obvious but don't we generally stop at this powerful realization without exploring what it is that we don't know … that insight or realization that just may hold the key to whatever it is we're struggling with?

If this is so, can we see that since we're generally unconscious of this powerful realization (that we don't know what we don't know) that reminding ourselves of this critical insight may prove difficult unless we devise a plan to remember it?

Well, one way to remind ourselves is to use any undesired situation we find ourselves in as a trigger to remind us that there must be something we aren't presently seeing, that if we did see it, it would make all the difference.

Isn't logic and reason a beautiful thing?

Furthermore, how can we consciously live out the rest of our lives in such a way so that we no longer work against ourselves and against the laws of life that govern every single one of us?

Isn't that what we all want? Don't we all want the least amount of inner division and discord? Don't we want to enjoy this life and enjoy the company of those we care for most?

Of course we do. We are wired to want to be happy.

Are you ready and willing to inquire into every belief you have and every assumption you have in order to uncover your natural state of happiness?

What would that be worth to you?

Is there anything you aren't willing to look at that may be covering over what's naturally, already shining?

To be truly happy you must become more conscious than you are right now. Try as you may, there is no way around this.

Of course you have every right to achieve all your goals and dreams and find out if it brings you the happiness you desire. No one is saying don't go for what you want in life.

By all means, go for what you truly desire in this life! I'm certainly not suggesting that accumulating all that you desire is a bad thing.

There's nothing inherently wrong with accumulating material possessions. It's when we believe that that particular object will make us happy.

If you set it up this way (if this is your view) then prepare for the emotional rollercoaster ride that is your life.

There can be no real and lasting happiness in that which is impermanent. It's literally not possible.

I don't care how much money you have in the bank or how many possessions you surround yourself with or how luxurious you live – you're kidding yourself if you don't think it could all be washed away like a sand castle at high tide.

History shows this again and again. And while it makes for "difficult" times, it's actually good news for your happiness because you can choose to consciously SEE this illusion for what it is – and free yourself from the agony of chasing a thing that must inevitably die out.

Seeing that everything is impermanent, we see that we set ourselves up for failure when we seek permanent and lasting happi-ness when we acquire things and experiences that are impermanent.

It is totally appropriate to enjoy things and experiences – just be aware that it will have a certain life span and can't ever give you lasting happiness independent of circumstance and condition.

You can choose to consciously see this NOW and free yourself from the agony of chasing this illusion once and for all.

But first, you must want to see it in order to be free of it.

Henry David Thoreau was an American author, poet and philosopher. He hit the nail on the head when he said:

"Happiness is like a butterfly: the more you chase it, the more it will elude you, but if you turn your attention to other things, it will come and sit softly on your shoulder."

Once the novelty of that new and shiny thing wears out (and it will because it must) what will you do then? Typically, you set your sights on another new and shiny thing, right?

It's a never-ending cycle. Do you really want to live your life this way, like a dog chasing its tail?

Is it just materials things we seek to fill the void inside? Don't we also seek to fill the void inside with other things like sex, drugs, alcohol, food, sleep, television, video games, going to the movies and even cigarettes?

How about seeking approval from others? Can you ever be truly happy seeking approval from others?

Heck, we could come up with a much bigger list, but you get the point.

There's nothing inherently wrong with any of those activities. Aside from cigarettes, alcohol and drugs, I enjoy every one of them.

It's when we use those activities as a means to temporarily escape the unhappiness we feel inside that it becomes problematic.

We seek to forget ourselves and to take the focus off of ourselves, don't we? Don't we want to forget about our struggles, even for a short while?

Getting a reprieve from our life is our goal. Sometimes, we even become addicted to these activities, only making matters worse and strengthening its hold on us.

This book wouldn't be complete if I didn't mention this:

If you're presently using drugs and/or alcohol and you KNOW that it impacts your well being, just be aware that you're literally trading these temporary behaviors that must lead to unhappiness ... for the chance of real and permanent happiness.

This trade off seems so obvious yet it took me years to see this very simple truth!

Additionally, if you use stimulants of any kind to excess, like caffeine or whatever, consider that your body must be at rest before the mind can be at rest – for they are one and the same.

It's also worth mentioning that absolutely NONE of this is cause for beating yourself up, especially if you want to uncover your natural state of happiness.

If you beat yourself up over what you're actually doing (reality) you will keep in place the VERY behaviors you want to remove.

Instead, just notice it without resistance or judgment and intend for something else, something more desirable. This is SO essential.

Okay, let's move on from drugs, alcohol and any other stimulants that must lead to unhappiness.

Since you can only understand what you are first aware of, you see that there must be something you aren't noticing that's causing any pain or dis-ease you may be experiencing.

Drawing conclusions (when you don't know what's true) limits and confines you because the truth often is something other than what you think it is.

Actually, since the truth is prior to thoughts or words – and what is being pointed to, it can never be what you think it is.

Become aware that your mind will attempt to tell you that there must be some thing (or group of things) that you can possess or activities you engage in that can make you happy for the rest of your life. If you only had that thing, you'd be happy. If you only could engage in those activities, you'd be happy.

You may even conclude that most wealthy people seem to be happy so money and a more comfortable lifestyle must be what you need to be happy.

Despite how strongly you may believe this, it just isn't true. There are many unhappy, wealthy people in this world – they just have bigger holes to fill because they, too, spend their attention and energy towards trying to fill the hole that can never be filled.

Now they may have the ability to put bigger and more expensive things in the hole they feel inside

– and engage in any and all the activities money can buy, but the same law applies to them.

Their hole cannot be filled, either. It too, is a bottomless pit, just like my brother-in-law, Chuck's stomach!

When you set it up in your experience that lasting happiness is found in loving things and using people, you're looking in the wrong direction. You'll never experience the happiness you seek. Never.

Happiness doesn't need any "thing" to be happy.

Again, it's when we think that a particular object will make us happy is where we go wrong, where we delude ourselves.

Happiness just is, right here and right now, patiently waiting for you to realize it literally needs nothing.

Happiness stands alone, all by itself, naked and free.

You certainly have every right to be rich and happy – and enjoy any experience you want on this beautiful planet, but in order to be happy you don't need to be rich.

Since everything changes (including your experiences) see the insanity of trying to permanently fill the apparent hole felt with things and experiences that must change.

Until then, happiness must elude you.

Chapter 3
Investigate What You Hold As True

Investing the time and energy to look at what you hold true is one of the single most powerful and transformative things you can ever do.

In fact, there aren't many things that can have a greater impact on your life and the lives of those around you than consistently doing this one thing.

This isn't always a quick and easy thing and can take a good bit of attention and persistent looking, but the rewards are well worth the time and energy invested.

Like many things in life, it's a process, a journey, but one well worth it.

It's rather simple actually, but not necessarily easy. If it was that easy, we'd be living in a much happier and kinder world, don't you agree?

You must be willing to look in places you may not want to look, despite any fear or reluctance that may arise.

This is what stops most people from making the breakthroughs they desire. Fear. Most people erroneously conclude that since they feel a thing (like fear) that it must be real, otherwise it wouldn't be present in their experience.

They also conclude – without knowing whether it's true or not – that the fear will be too much for them to handle. Putting your feelings aside for the moment, is that really true?

Courage has been defined as "acting in spite of the fear you may feel," so if you feel you must summon courage, then by all means, summon courage.

One of my favorite lines in a movie happened to be in my favorite movie, "Brave Heart."

When young William Wallace's father lay dead after battle, William dreamed that his father opened his eyes saying to him, "Your heart is free, have the courage to follow it."

It sent chills down my spine and touched me deeply because it resonated within that we're here on earth to follow the heart, no matter what our minds believe. We are here to express and enjoy ourselves and give ourselves to each other.

We are here to live out (and live from) what we have determined is our purpose in life.

Your mind thinks it knows the way when all along, your heart knows the way.

You can trust it, you really can.

Here's a useful suggestion: Since we make everything up anyway, consider setting it up within yourself that your desire to uncover your natural state of happiness is significantly more important than believing in the reality of the fear you may experience.

Secondly, don't assume that any fear that may arise is more than you can handle. It isn't if you (say and declare) that it isn't.

It's like when you have the perspective that the person you're arguing with is significantly more important than the topic you're arguing about.

With this perspective, what are the odds of the argument getting full blown and nasty? Not real high, right? Wouldn't it be more of a "spirited debate" than a testy argument?

Knowledge is found above the neck and wisdom resides below the neck.

If this is true (it most certainly is) then why do we keep looking for truth and happiness in our minds? It's not there, nor does happiness arise from there.

Happiness and wisdom both arise from below the neck, but don't take my word for it.

If wisdom resides below the neck in our hearts (being) then why do we keep looking to our minds for wisdom? Why do we constantly go to our minds to look for the answers when all along we know in our hearts what that "answer" is?

Almost all the time, FEAR can be an acronym for false evidence appearing real.

Just because you feel fear doesn't mean it's real, does it?

Since when have your feelings been a barometer for what's true and real? Isn't it almost always worse in our minds than the actual reality? It sure is.

Like everything else in this world, fear is just energy. Everything, including you, is just energy.

The earth is energy, the sun and the stars are just energy.

Thoughts, beliefs and feelings are energy. Your car and home is made of energy and the food you eat is energy.

If you are intrigued by this check out quantum physics. It will have you question everything you hold as true.

Quantum physicists have proven that absolutely everything is energy, vibrating at different frequencies, blinking in and out of existence all the time.

Also, the very fact of our observation and how we observe a thing changes that thing and changes how it behaves.

Here's something you may not have considered before yet we touched on it in chapter one: Almost every belief and assumption you have was never created by you.

You have (unintentionally) assimilated all your beliefs and assumptions from your upbringing and society in general.

Can you imagine the implications of this one insight?

If you don't believe this (or are unaware of this) be willing to take a real hard look at the vast majority of beliefs, assumptions and opinions that are guiding your life right now and trace them back as far as you can go.

You'll discover one of two things: that you are not the author and you never were. You literally picked them up along the way, from someone or somewhere, like a cross-country truck driver that habitually picks up hitch- hikers.

And the other discovery – if you're totally honest with yourself – is you just don't know where they came from.

Once you've confirmed this in your own experience, you can drop the beliefs that don't serve you. Because you brought them out of the darkness and into the light of your conscious awareness, they will dissolve spontaneously – or at worst, gradually.

Now you're able to consciously choose the perspective that serves you and those you most love and care about. You DO NOT have to be at the mercy of your beliefs anymore.

Until then, I'm afraid the only option is to live out your life based upon the conditioning you've unconsciously taken on ... and on what you believe to be true.

Consider the ramifications of discovering what you truly value and what your expectations of life and those around you are.

Do you actually expect to be happy and do you expect good things to come your way?

If you don't, how might your life be different if you woke up each day expecting to be happy and expecting to make valuable contributions to the lives of others?

Since we get what we expect in life, expect to be happy and expect others to enjoy your company.

Expect to be healthy, happy and successful and watch what unfolds in your experience.

Again, do you see that it's what you aren't aware of right now that must be the key to uncovering your natural state of happiness?

If you find yourself desiring more happiness, then doesn't it make sense that you must be unaware of something very significant that isn't presently in your field of conscious awareness?

Becoming more conscious of your habit patterns and tendencies is the first step to understanding them. Until then, you are destined to live out your days much like Bill Murray in Groundhog Day.

If you haven't seen the movie, I highly recommend you do so. It's funny, insightful and very inspiring.

It's been said that you can find out what you actually value by noticing where you invest your time and energy –and not what you say you value.

Often, what we say and what we do are two very different things.

For example, if you say you really value doing volunteer work or being kind to others, do your values match what actually manifests in your life?

Do you do volunteer work and are you actually kind to others?

You can say you value a certain thing but if it's not a reality in your life, then you probably don't really value it.

Most likely, you value the idea of it and not the actual experience of it.

Most people would be very shocked at many of the beliefs they have that they don't even know they have – and just how these beliefs show up in their lives.

For instance, do you believe you're incomplete? Do you really need that some thing or some one to make you feel fulfilled and complete?

If so, what tells you this? Is it a belief that tells you this?

What would you say if I told you that you're already complete and that it's just a thought that tells you otherwise?

Stop believing the thoughts in your head because despite feeling true, they aren't true! They aren't even close to the truth and they aren't even yours to begin with.

Have you ever wondered what a belief is anyway? Can we further dissect this thing called belief?

In a nutshell, beliefs are mental constructs created in the mind as a substitute for when we don't know what's true.

The majority of beliefs are spontaneously created (by the mind) in order for the mind to feel safe and in control – and to help you navigate and negotiate in this world.

Have you noticed yet that most beliefs you hold weren't consciously chosen by you? This is very cathartic to see.

Can you remember the day you decided to create the beliefs that you presently operate from? Of course you don't remember because aside from a few here and there, you never did it.

Don't believe me when I tell you that it is in fact your beliefs, assumptions and opinions that suppress the happiness you desire.

Don't believe me when I tell you that what others think of you is none of your business. Rather, find out for yourself, in your own direct experience if this is true.

Allow me to remind you not to use (and approach) this book like all the others you've read in the past. The beauty is, is that this is a fresh, new moment to see if what you believe is actually true.

This is a fresh, new moment to notice how often your natural tendency is to create beliefs in your mind versus actually finding out what's true in your experience.

And if we don't know what's true, are we willing to admit that we just don't know? Can we admit that often times, we can't know?

It is in THIS space that pure potential and limitless possibility loves to play! It is in THIS place where our freedom lies.

Again, the truth is, beliefs, assumptions and opinions are substitutes for when you don't know what's true.

Your mind doesn't like the unknown. It likes what it thinks or believes it already knows and then compares, contrasts and evaluates everything in relation to that.

Beliefs lock us into a certain way of perceiving that filters reality... like a veil that conditions our actual experience of life.

Humans invest way too much stock in their beliefs and opinions, beliefs and opinions that typically lead to what we don't want.

Have you noticed that belief often likes company – even seeks out company? Don't we feel comfortable and safe when we're in the company of those that believe as we do?

Truth stands alone and needs no company. And unlike most belief, it doesn't need any defending.

There's an inner knowing – where absolutely no doubt is present, that allows truth to securely stand all by itself, that needs no confirmation or validation.

Find that place and the ballgame is over.

Don't we actually believe that our opinions and judgments have so much significance, especially to ourselves?

Isn't it my belief versus yours?

And naturally yours is right and mine isn't.

Don't we often want another to see that we're "right" and don't we often want another to "come to our side" and agree with our perspective, the "right" perspective?

How many millions of people have been killed in the last 2000 years over differences in belief? How many wars have been fought, how much blood has been shed over my belief vs. your belief?

If one believes that this world is full of dishonest, selfish people, one will experience mistrust and have their guard up at almost every instance.

If one believes oneself to be on the receiving end of repeated mistreatment, then one will undoubtedly feel like a victim and expect to be mistreated at every turn.

Now I'm not saying that all beliefs are bad or wrong, nor am I implying that you should attempt to do away with them altogether, so please don't infer this.

Some beliefs are very useful and even serve as a way to protect you from harm. Some beliefs can act as a bridge, bringing you from where you are to where you really want to be.

For example, if you feel you're doomed to a life of unhappiness – even believe you won't ever be happy – you'd do well to turn that around and come to believe that you do deserve to be happy – and to believe that no human is more or less than you.

I don't know for sure (I can't know for sure unless I did it) if I were to drive a racecar around a track at 175mph whether I'd crash into the wall or not.

Since I don't have any experience (frame of reference) driving a fast racecar, I would lean on the side of caution and believe that I probably would lose control and crash.

Call me a wimp, but I'd probably pass on the opportunity.

If you really desire to improve your lifestyle and you want to become a self-employed entrepreneur instead of working for others – and you want to double or triple your income, believing that you can achieve this goal is very empowering.

In fact, you could say it's critical in order for you to put into action your plan of achieving that specific goal.

So let's not throw the baby out with the bathwater...

Not all beliefs are a disservice to you. Not all beliefs lead to undesired outcomes. The key is to be vigilant and aware of those that serve you and those that don't.

However, when it comes to being authentically happy, unexamined beliefs and assumptions rarely, if ever, serve you – especially if you aren't the happiest camper around to begin with.

If you want to experience the happiness you deserve, then strap on that spotlight of conscious awareness around your head (it's already there, just use it) and look to see the beliefs and assumptions you're currently operating from.

Don't be misled into believing that it's a painful, arduous and fearful thing to do. Yes, fear may come up, but so what? Don't let that stop you. It's just energy and nothing more – I promise, you won't die.

If you need to create a belief that says, "God won't ever give me something I can't handle"... then by all means, latch onto that belief and use it as means to get you through that challenge.

And always remember, you almost always get what you expect.

In the absence of belief, there is clear seeing and openness, infinite potential and possibility.

The late Zen Master Suzuki Roshi said it best: "In the beginner's mind, there are many possibilities. In the expert's mind, there are few."

See that the seeming hole inside is created by a belief in lack and incompleteness.

You have free will to believe anything you want and you also have free will to investigate and see what's really true, too. It depends on the kinds of experiences you really want to have.

The key aspect here is to be honest with yourself and admit that if you believe it, it means that you don't really know if it's true or not – and then proceed accordingly.

Lastly, the willingness and courage to NOT KNOW is essential if we want to uncover the happiness that is already shining, right here and right now.

Chapter 4
Argue With Reality And Suffer

BRICK WALL →

HEAD →
(FULL OF REALLY
BLOODY RUDE
WORDS)

FLUFFY POMPOM THINGS

Reality can be described as that which is actually occurring in any moment. Reality is what is.

In other words, what is means what's actually happening before your mind labels it as good or bad, positive or negative.

No doubt you've heard the popular saying these days, "It is what it is?" The true meaning of this phrase is that a thing, situation or event "is what it is" before the mind labels it as good or bad, positive or negative.

One of the most effective ways to suppress your natural state of happiness is to go to battle with what is – or what is actually occurring.

Do you want to be right … or do you want to be happy? I can report from my past experience (and you can, too) that often times when I was "right" I was also unhappy!

The only problem you ever really have is to want something to be different than it is – or to want someone to be different than they are. Period.

Your mind will argue that it can't be that simple! Your mind will tell you that things can be different than they are and things should be different than they are, but is this really true?

Can anything ever be different that it is in that moment?

Can it?

If you really see this (that the mind's main function IS to argue with reality) I can tell you that you're way ahead of more than 99% of the world's population.

REALLY.

Argue with reality and suffer – only every time.

Argue you with reality and you bang your head against a brick wall.

Yes, things are very often different than they were but are they ever different than they are?

Seeing the truth and simplicity of this can radically change your life. And the really cool part is that once you really SEE this, you can never go back to the old way of seeing.

Sure, this (resisting what is) will still come up in your experience but you don't believe it anymore. Since you don't believe it, it doesn't hang around in your experience for long. As a result, you won't suffer, either.

I chuckle inside every time I hear someone say that their favorite sports team "should have" won that game!

Depending on the degree and intensity, resisting what is can only bring discomfort, dis-ease, pain and/or suffering.

Notice what happens when you would like to have a different experience from the one you're actually having.

Have you ever considered IF it's even possible to have a different experience than the one you are having?

No really, have you?

If the thought that it's possible to have a different experience than what you are having is entertained, then it looks as if you can change it into something more desirable.

And this is where the train leaves the track, often traveling right over the gorge, falling hundreds of feet to the thick, dense jungle below.

As soon as you don't want the experience you are having, the not wanting is also an experience (with another layer) added onto your experience.

This layer of resistance leads to a contraction you feel in relation to what is actually happening.

You cannot escape this contraction if you resist what is – it must manifest because to put it simply, this is the way it works.

We seldom ever consciously examine (or notice) this contraction we feel in the body – and consequently, unconsciously believe that if we resist a thing that we don't want, it will actually help us in some way.

We tell ourselves that we can't just passively let (what we don't want to happen) to just happen without a fight.

We believe that to struggle against something will somehow protect us from what we don't want to experience, shielding and protecting us in some way.

The reality is, that when we resist what is, we reinforce it and lock it into our experience.

We actually reinforce that which we don't want to experience.

It's like we're banging our head into a brick wall thinking it will help us feel better.

The VERY interesting part is that we rarely ever verify this strategy to see if it's actually true in our experience.

Again, please don't believe me, but please do check it out in your own direct experience. It's very easy to do.

Most people haven't a clue as to what causes suffering.

Resistance to pain causes suffering. You may have heard that pain is inevitable, but suffering is optional?

As human beings, from time to time we will inevitably experience pain. It comes with the package of being human.

Pain is an inherent aspect of the finite, physical experience.

If pain wasn't a potential experience, could you experience happiness and joy?

Nope.

If we understand and live in harmony with the laws that govern us (that we cannot escape), pain can be minimal and short lived.

If we see that pain and happiness are two sides of the same coin and that we cannot experience one without the other (like life and death and hot and cold) we can allow whatever is happening to happen.

You already know this because you experience this all the time.

You can't have one without the other.

Notice how often your mind tells you that whatever is presently happening shouldn't be happening or that it could be happening differently. Has this ever been true in your life?

Or how about when your mind tells you that you "should have known" better and consequently done better? Based on your awareness at that moment in time, can that ever be true?

Can it?

If you're greatly impaired with a health challenge (or disease) that's progressively worsening ... and can't do most of the things you could before, what must be your experience if you resist what is?

Granted, you won't be happy about the situation, but you can certainly be at peace about it.

Why not enjoy the rest of your life in peace and let go to the fact of your condition instead of wishing things were different than they are?

If you say, "It's not that easy Alex, you try being in my shoes." I'd have to agree with you and perhaps say, " I hear you, I really do...and I have great compassion for you, but what's your alternative?

How do you want to spend the rest of your days?"

It's a fork in the road (we're at again, literally in each moment) where we can either reject or accept what is. Our perspective makes all the difference.

So feel what you feel, process it on your timetable and then let's get on to accepting the reality of the situation if we want peace.

Granted, this perspective of accepting what is doesn't always happen right away, so please understand that appropriately, there's a great deal of compassion for you if you face this particular situation.

Many things in life involve a process of coming to terms with the reality of what is – and this situation certainly applies. Upon receiving news we'd rather never get, who among us responds with, "Oh great, this is just what I hoped for!"

If your current job or career really sucks, fully accept that you have it now (want what you have) ... especially IF you aren't actively looking for another one.

Or, fully accept that it's your job or career now, without resisting it now, as you happily look for another one. Imagine the energy you bring when you are interviewing for another position.

Do one or the other, but only if you want to be happy.

Do one or the other, but only if you care about how you impact those around you that you love.

Besides, carrying around this type of energy will open way more doors than if you hate what is. Don't you already sense this?

I can't tell you how "guilty" I was of doing the above, the majority of which occurred in my twenties. I say "guilty" (not in terms of blame or shame) because I wasn't aware that my perspective of resisting reality was creating the suffering I didn't want.

Today, I can look back in amusement at the fact that it seemed to take forever to see how this law of life worked, especially since I got such immediate and direct feedback.

Apparently, I was very asleep and not ready to see what was true, until I was – and not a moment before.

If you've experienced a fair amount of pain and unhappiness in your life up to this point, you can choose to experience its opposite – happiness – for the remainder of your days.

Fully accept that you've experienced your life this way (and that it couldn't have been any different) and then choose to experience the other side of the coin, that is, the happy side.

But first, you must become aware and conscious of how you've created your experience up to now … and then intend for a more desirable experience by living in harmony with the law of your experience.

Just by being curious, open and nonjudgmental, we can be scientists in a lab experimenting with our direct experience and discover exactly how our experience is literally created.

We finally SEE that it's ALL an inside job, always and in all ways.

Can you think of a more worthy undertaking than learning how these laws that govern life work in your life – and then to actually cooperate with them?

Our lives become so much more enjoyable when we willingly abide by the laws of life.

Remember, you're playing to win, right?

The good news is that each moment gives us the opportunity to see this. Each moment gives us a fresh opportunity to see what's really true for us.

History does not have to repeat itself. You do have the power – and it's with your conscious awareness.

We can verify (in our experience) that when we don't want that pain, if we push that pain away, we feed it and keep it in place … and ultimately suffer.

Where your attention goes, energy flows.

Trust in life's intelligence and trust in your own being for they are one in the same. Even though your being and life's intelligence may appear separate, they aren't. You are Life itself.

The appearance is not the reality. It never is.

If we recognize and accept that pain is a fact of our existence, we can allow for pain to be our experience. We know that if we resist it, we give it continued life.

We see that by resisting anything, we are owned by it.

Pain is not the enemy and it never was! Your resistance to the pain was the problem. Pain itself is never the problem.

Allow what is natural do its thing. Pain is a natural energy of emotion and if we just let it run its course, it will not hang around and torture us.

We can see that all emotions are like the weather – they come and go. Stop feeding your painful emotions with resistance, accept that it arises and see what happens.

Watch that storm pass quickly.

When it was finally seen how this law was operating in my own life for almost twenty years, I knew I could intend for a much different experience.

I realized that I was literally a hamster on a wheel, unaware that not wanting the pain kept the wheel of suffering in motion! I was unaware that I was feeding (and giving life to) that which I did not want to experience – and my experience told me so.

I was working against myself when all along my body was telling me what was true, prodding me to work with life and not against it.

Trust the innate wisdom of the body – it knows and never operates from belief.

I truly cannot remember the last time I suffered. Why would I suffer anymore when I know what causes suffering?

Allow the pain to wash through you, allow it to run its course in its time (not yours) and watch how quickly it dissolves.

It's all energy. It will amaze you, I promise. The truth is simple, so simple in fact that your mind cannot comprehend it.

Stop believing it has to be complex in order to be true. See that the mind deals in complexity – and rarely simplicity.

Stop arguing with reality and strip away this particular unneeded layer that covers over your natural state of happiness.

No more sabotaging yourself – you deserve to be happy. It is your birthright.

Even if you notice a preference arise for something else, offer that no resistance ... and notice your experience.

Would you like a real simple formula for being at peace ... peace that leads to happiness?

Allow what is to be exactly as it is.

Chapter 5
What You Run From Can Only Chase You

Have you noticed that running away from a particular problem in your life typically makes it worse?

Don't we have a tendency to think that by *not* dealing with something (that causes us pain) it will hopefully go away?

Intuitively, we know that the exact opposite is true so *why* do we continue to do it? Why don't we *do* what we *know* to be true?

It was the apostle Paul who once said, "I do not understand what I do, for what I want to do I do not do, but what I hate I do."

For starters, don't we fail to take it one step further by examining what happens if we allow our experience to be as it is?

There's so much waiting for you if you do this one simple thing.

Also, isn't it in our make-up to avoid pain? Won't we usually go to any lengths to avoid pain and gain pleasure?

This isn't wrong or bad – it just doesn't ultimately serve you. You could say it's in our DNA to swim against the current of life at times, so don't go blaming yourself.

We're often like salmon swimming upstream to spawn when it's so much easier for *us* (and less draining) to go with the flow of the current of life.

Instead, why don't we row, row, row our boat, gently down the stream ... merrily, merrily, merrily ... life is but a dream.

To flow with life means to accept what's actually occurring in any moment.

We go against the flow until we don't anymore, until we see (in our experience) that swimming upstream doesn't actually serve us, until we see that going against life *brings us* suffering.

Call it cause and effect if you like.

We're wired to avoid pain and gain pleasure. Knowing this, why beat yourself up about it? Beating yourself up is another form of running and will keep the energy (that you don't want) in place.

Running IS resistance. Running *from* anything creates a negative energy that has nowhere to go and therefore, *must* stay with you.

What might happen if you take an approach of curiosity, without any judgment at all? What would that energy look and feel like?

Is it closed, limited and imprisoning – or open, spacious and free?

Which energy (approach) do you think will actually serve you? Which further imprisons you?

Do you sense that the path of least resistance comes from your own inner wisdom that is sensed below the neck?

Or do you sense the "smart way" of trying hard with lots of strain and effort that comes from a thought in your head, above the neck?

Do you sense that the truth is simple and not difficult?

Naturally, curiosity and wonder doesn't conclude and therefore, pigeonhole, limit and confine, does it?

Wouldn't you agree that cultivating a non-judgmental attitude allows what is to be *as* it is?

Someone once said, "You don't define others with your judgment; you define yourself as a person needing to judge."

Instead of continuing this unconscious pattern that invariably leads to unhappiness and suffering – and because you want happiness – why not intend to cultivate the habit of facing and embracing that which causes you pain – and see what happens?

Have you ever really done this? If so, what was your experience?

That which we face and embrace must dissolve and leave our experience. This is law - this is the law of your being in any moment.

Hey, don't believe me, okay?

You're a scientist in a lab experimenting with this insight, seeking to prove it true in our experience, right? Don't believe anything until you prove it true in your own experience.

If you *can't* prove it at first, be okay with *not* knowing. Admit that you don't know in that moment.

It really is okay not to know! What does it feel like not to know? Isn't there an open, spacious feeling present?

If there isn't, then you must be listening and believing in the concepts and opinions of what your mind is telling you.

We've been conditioned to believe, like Pavlov's dogs, that *not* knowing isn't a good thing. Like we're stupid or something...

And it's a big crock of you know what.

The unknown is nothing to be afraid of and certainly nothing to be ashamed of.

The unknown is more beautiful and peaceful than you can imagine.

You already know what the known gets you – so relax into the unknown – this is where your freedom is found. This is where your freedom is waiting.

The truth is, you're already free.

Here's the crucial thing you must see if you no longer want to be jerked around by the all those UN-useful, UN-serving beliefs in your head.

Some beliefs serve you, many don't. The trick is to find out first what you believe in – and then see if it serves you or not. If they don't, then discard them like you would a winter coat on a warm, summer day.

Also, know that it's okay to have a belief as long as you admit to yourself that you really don't know – or you wouldn't believe.

If you find yourself running from the unknown, what can only happen? You guessed right. The unknown will freak you out *and chase you at the same time.*

What's the antidote? Stop running from the unknown. Turn around and face what you don't presently know.

In fact, if you really inquire within, you'll discover that you don't know much at all. It is in *this* state of discovery… in *this* fresh, new moment where true joy is revealed.

Anything else is just conceptual knowing and conceptual knowing has no real power.

It's all an inside job and it always was. See that you're *already* part of the whole and that nothing is separate from you, despite any appearance to the contrary.

Sure, we are different and distinct from each other but the essence of what we are is exactly the same. Physical bodies are separate but what's animating them isn't separate.

Did your mind just have something to say about that? Do you believe it?

You'll be pleasantly surprised and even relieved, at what happens when you cultivate this new habit in your life.

At first, you'll need to be conscious of your present habit patterns in order for them to be old habit patterns.

You see *how* they were sustained and reinforced for so long and it became a way of being. Running away from things we'd rather not face is human nature after all – but does it *ever* really give us the experience we really want?

No, it doesn't.

Does it strengthen what we don't want?

Yes, it sure does – so see what's true and be free.

Eventually it will become automatic and it will become a habit pattern that happens all by itself. You aren't really "doing" anything here so don't fall into the trap of believing that this takes a lot of effort and strain.

It *does* take a willingness to look and inquire into what's really true. It does take a good bit of awareness and intent, but it doesn't take much effort – and it certainly doesn't require straining.

If happiness is indeed your natural state (it is) does it make much sense that we must effort and strive for what's natural, spontaneous and effortless?

It's not that your natural state of happiness wasn't present – it's just that it has been covered over with so many layers of untruth that you can't feel it, sense it.

Avoid nothing if you want real happiness. Avoidance is another form of running that can only chase you.

Do you agree that it's very possible we have dreams of being chased *because* we do so much running away in our lives?

When you know that everything must die, including the worm that's eaten by the bird in order to survive, you realize, "My God, I can cling to nothing. But I can enjoy what I have and when it goes, I'm no longer surprised because I know that I can't hold on to anything, including my own life and those I love dearly."

What is born must die. The body is born so the body must die.

Are you the body or do you *have* a body? Can you see the difference? It's extremely important.

At the risk of sounding strange or creepy, I must be honest with you. As far back as I can remember, I've always been drawn to cemeteries.

Aside from the peace that's felt there, cemeteries are such an "in your face reminder" of how fleeting this human life really is.

When you know that death only happens to the body and not you, funerals and cemeteries aren't creepy at all. Sure, funerals are naturally very sad and we feel much grief, but we see that without death, there can be no life, either.

As I write this section, I'm in a cemetery watching a funeral procession of cars pass through on their way to the gravesite of a loved one.

I can't help but wonder whether or not the newly deceased ever discovered the key to genuine and lasting happiness, hopefully long before *this inevitable day.*

My family will tell you just how much I like these kinds of reminders. They may even tell you just how much they don't always appreciate these reminders quite the way I do!

I guess I can be more respectful of that, huh?

Aside from the wonder I'm feeling as I watch the hearse go by, I can't help but *also* feel the sincere gratitude for the wonderful experience of being human, no matter how short it may be.

When I see what's really true and offer it no resistance, I am free.

Relatively speaking, it will *soon* be your last day that must come.

Do you know *when* your day will come? *Can you know when* your day will come?

How might your life be different if you absolutely and without condition, welcomed the fact that your day soon must come?

You'd be mostly free from the fear of the fact (that along with everyone else) your body must die, wouldn't you? Would you be chased by this fear anymore?

Despite an occasional fearful thought that might arise, you wouldn't.

So why do so many of us run from what must inevitably happen by nature, by design? Why do many of us fear that which billions have already experienced before us – and what billions must experience after us?

Well, wouldn't you agree that it's mostly because we fear the unknown? If we can't comprehend or grasp something, we usually fear it, don't we?

Isn't it interesting, even fascinating, that human beings run from what's literally inescapable, like the fact that our body must die?

If we delve deeper, don't we really fear the idea of no longer existing and not that our body must die?

Can you verify that you will no longer exist after your body dies? No, you can't.

When we run from the idea of our own physical death and the death of those we love ... and when we run from conversations about death, we make our fears of what's natural seem even more real.

And then we fear not only death, but really living as well.

When we see that absolutely nothing lasts forever and that nothing is safe from physical death, we can allow what must happen to take its natural course – because it will anyway, whether we want it to or not.

When we see and accept that the grand design isn't accidental or haphazard, we are no longer chased and haunted by our own thoughts "about" it.

Here again (as it always presents itself) we are wise to see the wisdom of no escape, aren't we? I mean, especially if we want to be truly happy in this relatively short human life we get to live?

Once we can truly accept and trust this Grand Design, don't you think we are much better able to enjoy our lives – even be happy with our lives because we know it won't last forever?

When we see (that for the most part) we really don't have control over any of it, don't we give ourselves that ability?

Wouldn't this truth realized in our hearts set us free?

Face life as it is, not as you want it to be.

Life IS integral; it's ONE life. You can't separate bits and say, "Oh, that's unacceptable and this is okay." You've got to encompass all of it or you'll always suffer.

No avoidance. Stay right where you are.

Running away from anything covers over (and puts to sleep) your natural state of happiness, every time.

Strip those layers away and face what's facing you

Chapter 6
What You Do To Others You Do To Yourself

This is one of my favorite laws of happiness, probably because it's so obvious. It talks to you all the time, sometimes very loudly.

And it's very difficult not to hear it. It's very difficult not to feel it, too.

It even gives you immediate feedback in every moment and never leaves you.

Some laws of life are subtle and more difficult to sense than others.

This one isn't subtle at all. This one is right out in the open – inviting us to see just how simple and consistent it really is.

If everyone on the planet lived in harmony with this one obvious and consistent law, we'd surely have a much different planet.

We'd have a planet full of happy people with a vibration easily felt by those that weren't happy.

This law was revealed to me in my early twenties one day while I was being unkind to a girl-friend.

For some reason, it hit home (like a sledgehammer) that it was impossible to feel good about myself as I was mistreating her.

I can still remember the voice inside that said verbatim, "What you do to others you do to yourself."

This wasn't exactly an earth shattering revelation as I had always suspected this, but some-thing deeper happened.

Something energetic traveled from the thought (in my head) to the realization in my heart (being) that in order to be truly happy, I could not mistreat others.

You could say that real knowing finally happened (because it went from the head to the heart) and I knew that things would be very different than before.

In other words, I finally saw something hugely significant and something so profound yet simple, that I just knew that my life would never be the same.

I realized in that moment, that true knowing wasn't conceptual – that it could never be just conceptual.

I saw that "conceptual knowing" was basically a contradiction in terms. It was when you knew "about" something – much like philosophy, dogma or ideology.

The philosophy of happiness or the philosophy of spirituality is essentially "ideas about" happiness and "ideas about" spirituality and never, ever the actual.

Just as the word or concept is never the actual (can you drink the word "water" or be burned by the word "fire") philosophy is never the actual, either.

Philosophy can, however, act as a stimulus (or catalyst) that can spark a recognition or remembrance within of what was always and already known.

Then it moves from the conceptual to the experiential, becoming alive and organic in our experience.

It was from that day on that I realized to truly know something it had to be "known" below the neck and not above the neck. In other words, in order for anything to be truly known, it had to be understood and validated in my gut.

And that anything else (excuse the metaphor) was basically mental masturbation!

Gratitude washed through me as I knew this was truly a gift of grace and not something I did or deserved of my own accord.

The good news is that this law or principle is very easy to prove true. In fact, you can do it right now if you desire.

Imagine that you insult another person. How do you feel as you insult that person? Not too great, right?

Instead of imagining, go back in your memory to a time you mistreated someone. How did you feel as you mistreated them?

You'll find that it's literally impossible to feel good as you mistreat another, right?

It's pretty straightforward, don't you agree?

Have you ever fully realized that what you do to others, you do to yourself, too?

We go around forgetting this one simple thing, this one simple thing that makes such a huge difference in our experience – and the other's experience, too.

Similarly, when you hug someone in a genuine way, look another in the eyes and say something heartfelt ... or simply do a good deed without any expectation of receiving anything in return ...

How do YOU feel?

Pretty darn good, right?

This is different than the golden rule that says, "Do unto others as you would have them do unto you."

The golden rule is more of a commandment that tells rather than a law that demonstrates (shows) what you are, I am – and that I cannot escape or wipe my hands clean of how I treat another.

Pretty amazing isn't it? And it was right here all along, never hidden.

With this newfound insight, go out and truly be for others, do for others and see what happens.

Much of what causes our unhappiness is our belief in separation, our belief that there is a limited amount of resources to go around (scarcity mentality) and our belief that we must struggle to get what we want in life.

Therefore, instead of cooperating (heart) with others knowing abundance is the true reality, we compete (ego) with others because we believe that there isn't enough to go around, so we must get ours.

In short, we compete when we are ignorant of what's true.

How many of us actually test the assumptions that literally dictate our daily experience?

Seems like a worthwhile thing to investigate, don't you agree?

Do these assumptions and beliefs actually have significance or is it just a thought that tells you they're significant?

If we can only ever operate from our perspective of life, wouldn't it make sense to find out if our perspective is even true in the first place?

Wouldn't that be one of the most worthwhile things one could ever do, especially if one seeks to enjoy lasting happiness?

Wouldn't it?

If our perspective is based on separation, scarcity and the inevitable struggle – is it even possible not to project that onto those around us?

Here's the point: You cannot escape what you are and what you cling to as true. You cannot escape the effects of what you vibrate and since everything is energy, what you vibrate you must attract.

Therefore, embrace the wisdom of no escape and see that what you do to others, you do to yourself.

Now check this out. On the flipside, what you do to yourself you also do to others. It's a closed loop with nowhere to go but right where you are.

If you aren't happy with yourself and if you truly don't love yourself, it's virtually impossible not to consistently mistreat others.

I know someone personally who epitomizes this (don't we all) and unfortunately, she simply refuses to be willing to be honest with herself.

She refuses to take a good, hard look and see how she creates her own experience – and to see the inevitable and destructive impact she has on others.

In her mind, it's always someone else's fault. The finger is always pointing outward and like a boomerang, it all must come back, right to where it originated – from her perspective based on her beliefs.

And her experience of herself rarely ever changes. She'll forever be stuck on that wheel of suffering (unless and until) she has the desire and courage to look and see for herself.

What happens when you squeeze an orange? OJ must come out, right? Not apple juice, but OJ.

If you have bitterness and resentment in your heart and mind, what must come out? Conversely, if you have happiness and gratitude in your heart and mind, what must come out?

What you're vibrating at any moment is what must come out, only all the time.

Despite what you may believe, you cannot love another more than you love yourself.

If you want happiness, first find out why you aren't happy. It's so simple that your mind overlooks it.

Do not be deceived by the illusion of apparent separation. As no man is an island, absolutely nothing exists isolated from the wholeness of Reality.

If you believe you're an island unto yourself, then is it any wonder that you experience dis-satisfaction and lack?

The good news is that ALL OF THIS is in the past and doesn't have to be your experience in this fresh, new moment.

The question is, will you keep a dead thing (the past) alive? Will you repeat the same patterns over and over?

What about right now?

It's up to you and no one else.

Chapter 7
You're Most Present When You're Most Absent

Have you ever noticed that when your focus is off of yourself and your problems that you are most present and alive?   How does this *feel* and what is your experience when you aren't thinking about yourself?

Aren't you at peace when all this "stuff" is absent?

Aren't you very present in the moment, often without a care in the world?

Well, naturally!

How cool is that?

Isn't it also peculiar that we often think of ourselves first (and what we want) *before* thinking of others? Channel WIFM – what's in it for me?

Don't we also often wonder why we aren't nearly as happy as we would like to be?

Don't we sometimes wonder *how it is* that our friend or co-worker seems to be so happy when we aren't?

This is because me, me, me is a recipe for misery....

How do you think your life would be different if you didn't reference everything back to you?

How might things be different in your life if you realized that all your struggles were directly related to your habitual focus on yourself – and how absolutely everything impacted *you*?

See that the majority of your struggle in life stem from being self-absorbed and trying to fill the void inside with things external to you.

For the next week, consider trying a little experiment and commit to being in service to others. Commit to making others happy, whether it's with a kind word or a good deed.

Take careful note of the results. I bet it will be one of the most fulfilling weeks of your life. I bet you'll feel more present than you have in a long time – because you weren't absorbed with yourself.

If our main focus, energy and attention is about satisfying our own needs at all costs (and even sometimes at the expense of others) happiness must escape us.

I can tell you with the utmost assurance that those that are truly happy don't possess this me-first orientation.

It's literally impossible to have this "me-first" orientation AND be genuinely happy.

Truly happy people know without any doubt that there is no secret to happiness.

In fact, they know it's rather simple, open and available to all. They know that in order to be truly happy and free, they must live in accord with the natural laws of happiness that govern all of us.

Happy people aren't smarter (and know more) than unhappy people.

Most happy people are, however, consciously aware of (in tune with) what suppresses happiness, so in this sense you could say that they "know more" because they see something unhappy people don't yet see.

Whether this awareness was through years of being unhappy or not matters not.

They know it because they live *from* the laws (or principles) of happiness, now.

Why do you suppose so many people are drawn to meditation?

If done correctly, meditation can be a very effective tool in facilitating a reprieve from the dissatisfaction we experience on a daily basis – and even bring us temporary peace and happiness.

Don't misunderstand the point here. I'm not suggesting meditation isn't useful because it can be very useful.

Meditation (or sitting in silence as I like to call it) serves many purposes, one of which is to calm an overactive mind that can wreak havoc.

I have meditated quite a bit in the past and have discovered so much from this practice. However, what inevitably happens when you're no longer meditating?

After the usual short period of calm subsides, where your mind is pretty quiet and not telling you what's wrong and what's missing in your life, don't your "issues" typically come roaring back in?

Any practice (including meditation) has a certain life span. There is a beginning, middle and an end.

Likewise, any experience you have also has a beginning, middle and an end, too, does it not? In other words, it's temporary.

When your mind is focused primarily on itself – and all the things it deems unsatisfactory, *how can satisfaction ever be felt?*

How can we be happy if we believe we are incomplete?

Conversely, a mind that is still, a mind that *isn't* focused on itself and its problems leaves one feeling almost absent and as if they aren't there.

What is actually absent is all their life struggles – the struggles that dominate much of their existence.

The wonderful thing is that this is when "you" are most present. When you are no longer self-absorbed and referencing everything back to yourself, you feel absent but very much alive and present at the same time. And dare I say happy?

Yes, this is also when happiness arises, when you are most absent.

Discover this and be free from yourself, free from your mind that tells you that you must have this or that in order to be happy.

In this way, you free others as well.

You free them from *your* projections, *your* expectations and *your* judgments.

Allowing another to *be as they are* is truly a gift of giving and one that is always received with gratitude and appreciation.

Let us see what might happen in our experience if we change the order of the wording in this chapter title.

What if this chapter was called, "You Are Most Absent When You Are Most Present?"

I am not talking about disassociation here. That is an altogether different state, a state you may want to seek a therapist for.

What do you suppose would be *your actual and direct experience* if all your "problems" were absent in the present moment – or any moment for that matter?

And that in no way were you referencing anything back to yourself?

What if there was no resistance to what was actually occurring in any moment? In other words, you were cooperating (consciously or not) with Reality – or what is?

As you have probably have seen by now, you'd be very content, even happy.

You'd be happy because you know happiness won't arise, *can't* arise, when you're paying attention to what's missing in your life or what's missing in your experience.

It's just not possible.

When you become fully present in the only point of power, this now moment, your natural state of happiness must arise for this is law of presence, the law of your experience.

At the risk of having you roll your eyes, I have to repeat it. Don't believe a word you read here, but please do check it out_in your direct experience and validate for yourself whether this is true or not.

The power of your presence trumps absolutely everything, even unhappiness. Your presence is most powerful and radiant when the focus is off of your-self.

When you bring your full attention to this moment and take your focus off anything you may be discontent with, notice what arises.

This is where happiness is felt.

The past is memory and the future is imagined. Both are created in the mind. Despite what your minds says, the truth is, there's only now.

The more you consciously "do" this, the sooner it happens naturally and spontaneously – all on its own.

Talk about cool.

Knowing how it all works is the key but if you avoid the actual looking and willingness to experiment, nothing will change.

You can take this to the bank – it will pay out in dividends like you've never seen before, I CAN guarantee this one

Chapter 8
What You Pay Attention To

"I'm nothing, and yet, I'm all I can think about."

You've probably heard the saying, "what you focus on expands and grows stronger."

And that *what* you pay attention to *must* manifest itself in your experience.

If you pay attention to how sad you are, is it likely you'll feel happy? Is it likely you'll feel less sad?

If you pay attention to *all* the things you are grateful for, is it likely that you'll feel sad?

HECK NO.

If you focus on why you aren't happy and if you look at all the things that make you unhappy in your life, you become unhappier, don't you?

If you focus on what you don't have or what you feel is missing, you feel lacking and you feel incomplete, don't you?

If we pay attention to (and believe) a perspective that says we aren't complete, we'll naturally *feel* incomplete, right?

And since you can feel it, don't you almost always conclude that it must be true *because* you feel it?

What happens when we pay attention to a belief that says we aren't enough? Can we feel anything other than insecure and less than?

No, we can't.

What happens when you focus on the silence and stillness in between each thought you think and each word you speak?

Try this now please.

You become more still, don't you?

Did you confirm this for yourself or are you just reading concepts here?

If our attention gets caught up in thinking that we need to have a certain lifestyle to be happy, don't we feel a dissatisfied longing *until* that lifestyle is met?

Since what we focus on usually expands, don't we often get increasingly dissatisfied when we focus on what's missing?

Is it even true that something is missing? Or is it a thought or belief that tells you something is missing?

We get what we pay attention to, every time.

While much of this goes on unconsciously and without your intention, it doesn't have to continue to be this way.

We don't wake up each morning with the intent of feeling crappy that day, do we? It just happens this way, until it doesn't anymore.

It happens this way until we become aware that it's even happening – and then we can be aware of a new intent.

And then we can pay attention to acting in harmony with our new intent.

That is the beauty in all of this. The moment that just passed does not have to match the next moment. History does not have to repeat itself unless you remain at the same level of consciousness.

It was Albert Einstein who said, "Problems cannot be solved at the same level of thinking that created them." And he also said, "A man should look for what is, and not for what he thinks should be."

Here's what I know from my actual experience: when I notice something I'd rather not have in my life and offer no resistance to its presence, I see that it has a very short life span.

Since I'm already very aware (via my actual experience) that wanting something *other than what I've got* only feeds what I don't want, resistance rarely comes up.

If resistance does come up, it's seen almost immediately and let go of. Consequently, I am no longer in bondage to that thing.

Most of this happens automatically now but in the rare times that it doesn't, I know that there *must* be some resistance present or it would not be in my experience.

It's very simple actually, mostly because it's easily validated. It is felt energetically in the body and *this is its way of telling you* that you are in resistance to that thing.

If you listen and trust what your body is telling you – and allow what is happening to simply happen, it lets go. It must because you just took away its energy and life force.

Notice where your attention goes in each moment, because where your attention goes, energy flows.

Imagine that in *each* moment there is a fork in the road.

Going in one direction your attention is placed on what is actually happening – and being absolutely okay with what's happening.

In the other direction your attention and energy is placed on what you think *should* or *could* be happening.

If you were to come to this fork in the road – this fork that resides in each new moment – which direction will you travel if you want your desires met?

You got it, the side where there's no opposition to what is actually happening.

Don't believe me....

If you've read this far (and been in a state of open discovery and have been looking for yourself) I imagine that you are beginning to see – and feel – that there is no way to be genuinely happy if you argue with what is.

Please don't misunderstand what I am saying. This doesn't mean you must passively 'lie down' and be okay with anything and everything that comes your way.

Part of the wonder and joy of being human is that we will always have our unique likes, dislikes and preferences. That's part of being uniquely you.

Manifesting your likes, dislikes and preferences is your natural right.

This does mean, however, that if you want something to be different than it is, allow it to be exactly as it is *as you intend* for something more desirable.

It's not rocket science, is it?

How many of us were raised with this awareness?

Why energize and bring life to what you don't want?

In other words, thank whatever arises for appearing and then tell it you're grateful for it's appearance because it reminded you of what you REALLY want.

Use what you don't want as a trigger and accept its presence.

Use that newfound awareness as the springboard for what you really desire and watch what you desire come to you quicker than you ever imagined.

I also hope at this point that you *see* why I keep saying, "don't believe me <u>check it out</u> in your own direct experience."

I cannot stress enough the importance of actually *doing* these simple experiments and REALLY SEE FOR YOURSELF how you create your experience.

Otherwise, this will sadly just be another book you've read "about" the subject of happiness!

Don't let this book be just another set of concepts that you read "about" how to be happy.

I hope you don't use this book as just a temporary escape from your life, either. If you do, you can be sure that it's patiently waiting for you once you're done this book.

Use this book for which it is intended – to show you how to understand and abide by the rules (or principles) of happiness.

If you take on the experiments in this book and commit to following them through AS IF your life depended on them, you will uncover your natural state of happiness.

If you try to fix or change what is already occurring, what presently arises in your experience, happiness eludes you.

It must.

If our orientation is one of wanting more, better or different (while going to battle with what is) we are uneasy and not at peace.

When we put our attention towards allowing what is (to be just as it is) our experience is no longer one of contraction and limitation.

It is in this open spaciousness where no conclusions or judgments are made where happiness comes out to play, where happiness *only* likes to play.

Granted, much of the unhappiness we bring about happens automatically and unconsciously.

However, if we become aware of what we pay attention to in any moment, we're much less susceptible to falling into the trance-like states that flow from being unconscious.

Happiness doesn't like to come out and play when this happens.

Uncover Your Natural State Of Happiness

If your orientation is one of a deep contentment with what is actually occurring in any moment – and where nothing needs to be added or subtracted – you *will* experience a whole different reality.

You will because you must. This is the law of life.

So we do well to be mindful of the fact that wherever we place our attention and energy is what we literally ask for.

Only when we pay attention to what we pay attention to, do we give ourselves the opportunity to uncover our natural state of happiness.

Only when we pay attention to how we suppress our natural state of happiness can lasting happiness begin to be felt.

Chapter 9
Wanting What You Have

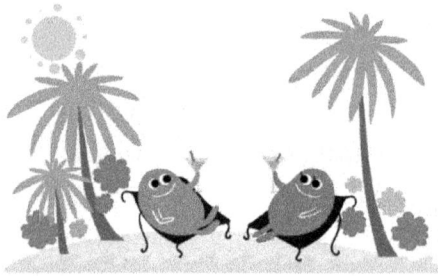

I remember back in college when I would go to the gym and work out. I was six foot two and about 175lbs – on the leaner side for sure. I wanted more muscle, especially in my legs! I'd look at the guys in the gym with the body parts I wished I had. No matter how much wishing or hoping, it never happened.

No matter how many exercises I did or amount of weight I pushed or pulled, I just couldn't duplicate what they had.

It bothered me and consequently, I felt insecure.

I failed to recognize that I would never have what they had, that I would always be uniquely me, with the body I was given.

The mind comes up with some of the most ridiculous notions that have nothing to do with reality! That isn't the problem though – *the problem is when we believe in and identify with those notions.*

I mean, if you told me back then that I'd never have what *that* guy had, I'd agree and even see how silly my wishing was.   We'd probably even have a laugh together.

Even still…the hoping and wishing would arise from time to time and I'd inevitably feel more insecure.

It wasn't until I really consciously saw how ridiculous it was for me to entertain (and identify with) the wishful comparisons that my mind came up with that it stopped happening.

When I saw what was *really* true – and when I was ready to fully accept that truth and its implications, liberation happened.   I no longer 'wished I had' what others had.

Today, I'm content and happy with the body I have, mostly because I know just how ridiculous comparing to others is – and where it must lead.

Besides, the human body is so amazing, with the ability to heal itself and do so many remarkable things.   The human brain is far more advanced than any supercomputer ever made.

Admittedly, from time to time I'll make fun of my calves and compare them to my brother in law's calves (yes, the one with the bottomless pit for a stomach) but it's all in fun nowadays.

There's one exactly like me in this world and there's no one exactly like YOU in this world. Celebrate this wonderful fact of existence and revel in the beauty of it!

Do you compare yourself with others? Have you ever looked to see if you do this?

Maybe you do it financially?

Maybe you find yourself trying to keep up with the Jones' and wish you had what they have?

Do you feel insecure about the car you drive or the home you live in?

How about the profession you're presently in, you know, the one where you spend about forty plus hours a week?

Do you wish you had the career someone you know has? Do you resist and bemoan the career you actually have? What's that experience like?

Do you compare your appearance with others? Do you wish you were more attractive than you are?

Do you believe you'd be happier if your significant other was more attractive than he or she is? Do you wish he/she was as attractive as your friend's partner?

I'm sure you see where I'm going here and the common denominator: you are resisting what is –

you're wishing for things to be different than they are – when you know it can never be different than it is.

Do you see just how crazy and silly your mind can be? Do you see how you mind really likes to mess with you?

Do you SEE that the mind doesn't give a HOOT about reality (what is) and that it often wants something other than reality?

And then you believe what your mind tells you?

Naturally, by law, this causes varying degrees of unhappiness. If you really take a look at it, it's literally insane.

Imagine someone coming up to you and complaining about how the sky is always blue. "It should be green!" they say. "Wouldn't that be better?!" And they spend their whole life wishing the sky was green instead of accepting the reality that it was blue all along.

You'd say that person was literally insane, wouldn't you? Or at the very least you'd say that person was totally delusional, right? Well, that's how most of us spend our lives, until we don't anymore.

Anytime we compare or demand that things be different than they are, we essentially tell ourselves that something isn't quite right and that something is indeed missing in our experience.

Can you ever be happy with this perspective?
Nope.

So why do we do this to ourselves?

Actually, you don't consciously (and intentionally) do this, unless of course you're a masochist.

Can I ask you a strange question? Are you a masochist?

Do you want to know *how* this is true – that you *don't* consciously intend for this to happen? Okay, I'll tell you.

Do you *decide* to oppose what's actually happening in any moment and then wish for it to be different than it is?

Or does it happen spontaneously and without your intention?

If you're honest with yourself, you'll see that it happens all on it's own. You'll see that it arises by itself without you deciding for it to.

This is what your mind does and it's up to you to notice it *and* its impact on your experience … BUT ONLY IF you want to be happy.

Resisting what is, is a form of insanity. Believing that anything *can* be any different than it *is* right now is insanity. Do you see this? I mean, really *see* this?

See the humor at how your mind just loves to compare and contrast, evaluate and judge… even to the point of making you miserable.

Even though most of us have been taught that others can "make us unhappy" the truth is, no one can make us miserable (including our own mind) *unless we give our permission.*

It's all an inside game. See this and be free.

Welcome all of it and laugh your butt off. Laughter is NOT resistance. Laughter doesn't feed what you *don't* want.

Laughter disperses and laughter dissolves what you *don't* want.

Have you ever seen a picture, figurine or statue of the laughing Buddha? He's laughing at the realization of the insanity of the mind – and its tendency to resist what's actually happening.

Curiosity, non-judgment and laughter are three medicines that will go a long way in uncovering your natural state of happiness.

But don't believe me.

You'll always be uniquely you and *never* will you be remotely close to another.

Consequently, you'll always have what you have, and never what another has.

Just as there are no two snowflakes or finger-prints that are identical, there will never be another just like you, ever.

Now isn't that beautiful?

Do you think this is by accident?

Can you imagine a world where we all looked very similar, had very similar capabilities, attained similar levels of success and had very similar challenges, likes and dislikes?

BLAH!

Diversity *is* beautiful, don't you agree? If you don't see the beauty and splendor *in* diversity, you *will* once you watch the 6-minute video at the end of this book.

If you don't, I suggest (like Kramer on Seinfeld) that you consider electric shock therapy, okay? Just kidding.

Do you believe that this (wide array of diversity) is just a random thing – or something part of a grand, order and infinite intelligence that's so far beyond what your finite mind can comprehend?

I invite you to look at the arrogance that says *you should be different than you are!* And to even entertain the notion that The Source or God (or whatever name you choose) got it wrong.

You are meant to be you, *just* the way you are. Geez, I just heard Billy Joel singing *Just The Way You Are* in my head.

You are designed specifically to have the certain set of skills and abilities, tendencies and personality traits that *only you* have.

Am I saying you can't cultivate other traits and abilities you would like to have? No, I am not. You *can* achieve almost anything you set your mind to.

What the mind can conceive the mind can achieve, right?

The key here is <u>want what you have</u> AS you seek to manifest something more desirable in your experience.

Wanting what you already have emits an energetic vibration of gratitude that can only attract more in like kind.

The other big key is to focus on what you want, *not* on what you don't want. I invite you to look at how often we focus on what we don't want.

Allow what is, be a lover of what is (as you happily intend for something more desirable) and you will effortlessly draw to you that which you truly desire, happily.

Temporary happiness arises when we get what we want. Lasting happiness arises when we want what we have.

And unless you're happy with who you are, you will never be happy with what you have.

Chapter 10
For The Highest Good Of All

Do you know people who are so transparent that it's easy to tell that they just don't want the best for others?

I am in my later forties now and I have yet to meet a person that is happy (that doesn't want) the best for others.

Conversely, I have met many unhappy people (who don't want) what's best for others. Some will even tell you!

It actually irks them when they see others, including "friends" or family succeed or benefit in any kind of way.

One reason for this is that unhappy people generally don't like to see others happy because it only increases their insecurity and dissatisfaction – and often validates their belief in their own perceived incompleteness.

Are you beginning to recognize how fragile and self-fulfilling minds can be?

There are those who even become increasingly somber when others are happy and content. Sadly, they fail to see that their VERY attitude is *the thing* that keeps their lives the same.

I worked as a house painter in college with a guy who had an established contracting business. He's basically a decent guy and definitely fun to be around when money isn't involved, but you just got the sense that he didn't want you to be more successful than him.

It's as if it threatened him and reminded him that he wasn't doing as well as he'd like to – and that as long as he was doing "better" than you, everything was good in his world.

He'd deny it to this day and even swear on his grandmother's grave. He still has the "I need to be more successful than you" attitude today – and unless he's willing to really see how this belief manifests in his experience, he'll likely take it to *his* grave.

There's nothing wrong with this. After all, it's his life and he can live it out as he wishes. It's just that it doesn't have to be this way.

However, it's a shame in a way because there truly *is* enough for all. The reality is that abundance is all around us and that we are literally bathing in it. Scarcity and lack is the illusion.

It is the mind that believes in scarcity and lack.

There's a huge difference in our experience when we come from a spirit of cooperation versus when we come from a spirit of competition.

Which do you live from?

If we aren't as happy as we would like to be, one way to be happier is to want the best for others.

Allow me to bring this point home further. No doubt you have heard of the law of attraction? It basically says that whatever we think about, we bring about.

Wherever we place our attention, we get more of that, whether we want it or not.

In other words, you are literally a magnet, drawing to you all that you entertain in your mind and emotions.

In fact, the more emotion and expectancy you have around a certain thing, the quicker you draw it in your experience, whether you want it or not.

This law or principle doesn't give a hoot whether you believe in it or not because it surely believes in you.

While there is much more to this law than I will go into in this book, I will say that understanding some of the basics can be very useful to you as you seek to reveal your natural state of happiness.

The reason I said in the prior chapter to focus on what you want and not on what you don't want is this:

If what you resist persists and if everything is indeed energy – including thoughts, beliefs and emotions, what do you suppose your experience *will inevitably be if you don't want what's best for others?*

You got it, more misery and scarcity for you.

Not wanting the best for others literally sends out a vibration of lack and limitation and you virtually tell the universe, "Give me more lack and limitation, please!"

If you want to be happy, be genuinely happy for others. If you think you can fool the laws of happiness, think again. Unless you truly want what's best for others, happiness will be as present as a deadbeat dad, as present as snow on a hot summer day.

On a more personal note, I was a pretty decent athlete growing up. While I enjoyed most sports, basketball was the main sport I excelled in.

I remember deriving much of my confidence (and self esteem) from the fact I was a good basketball player. Little did I know that I linked my esteem up to something that *had to* come to end one day.

Anyway, a few years after we moved into our new home in the early 1970's, my father had concrete poured over fifty percent of our backyard and my grandfather, a pipe fitter by trade, erected a ten-foot basket with three long pipes (a tripod) with plywood as the backboard. Finally, the basket and net was secured.

It was THE BEST basketball court in the entire town (it was huge) and so many kids came to play at my house, year after year! There was even a very bright halogen spotlight attached to the house so we could even play at night.

If you build it, they WILL come!

Sorry, I digress. I was reliving so many fun times as a kid for a few minutes there.

Anyway … since much of my identity was wrapped up in being a "good basketball player" there was naturally an underlying insecurity that went with it.

In fact, *there had to be* because being a good basketball player isn't a permanent and lasting thing. When I stopped playing, you can imagine the sadness and confusion I felt.

I still remember sensing that when I stopped playing, this experience would happen.

When we identify our self worth with that which is fleeting, that which comes and goes…. insecurity and discontent must arise.

I remember noticing that in my mid-later teen years it became very apparent that I had real difficulty complimenting others, whether on the basketball court or just in general.

Instead of just chalking it up to being super competitive, something else arose. I got real curious and wondered why it was so hard for me to praise people.

Was it just because I was so competitive and had to win at all costs? I soon discovered, after some digging, that I had a belief that told me I would be "less than" if I praised others.

This was my belief and I believed it hook, line and sinker. Do you think I was insecure? You bet I was.

Was my belief that I'd be "less than" (if I praised others) actually true? Heck no! Did it feel true?

YES, it sure did.

I would have gone on believing this untrue thought for years and years if I hadn't seen what was really true that one day.

It wasn't until much later that I discovered what had happened. When you shine the light of your own conscious awareness on anything (and bring it out of the shadows) it can't survive much longer.

In other words, when you meet anything with a welcoming awareness, it won't continue to hang around.

How cool is that?

I saw that if I wanted anything to dissolve or leave my experience, I was best served with a neutral and impartial looking – without emotion, resistance or judgment.

Anyway, from the age of about seventeen to my early thirties, I wasn't the happiest guy to be around. I couldn't help but spread that vibration, as it's truly a package deal.

In retrospect, I know that it could *not* have unfolded any differently than it did, despite how silly it seems now.

If you want to play by the rules and win, want the highest good for everyone you encounter.

If it's NOT authentic, then there's something you haven't seen yet. Keep looking inward.

You can't fool the laws, the universe, Nature, God, Jesus, Buddha, Your Higher Self or *whatever* you wish to call it.

Heck, call it "Fred" if you wish because you know the word isn't the actual.

Only the phonies don't get to uncover their natural state of happiness.

It's not possible to uncover your natural state of happiness if you don't want the best for others.

In fact, it's a very good way to keep it covered over.

Chapter 11
Be Responsible For Your Entire Experience

By Frits Ahlefeldt

For many years I went through life believing I was a victim, even convinced I was a victim. I was like Curly in The Three Stooges believing I was a "victim of coicumstance!"

I couldn't see that it was not the circumstances that got me down but rather my response to them that determined my experience.

I believed I was a victim of the circumstances as a result of my upbringing and my chemical makeup. My belief system even told me what I could and couldn't do.

I was pretty good at arguing for my limitations, too.

I even gave a fifteen-minute oral presentation in college on Epictetus, a Greek sage and philosopher who said, "It's not what happens to you, but how you react to it that matters."

I had a strong sense back then that I really was responsible for my entire experience, but I wasn't ready to really investigate and see if it was ultimately true or not.

Apparently I needed another twelve more years of unhappiness to be ready.

Interestingly enough, there wasn't much denial present about my experience in life; I'd tell you *exactly* what was wrong with my life.

I was that over-share, TMI guy (too much information) and shared my misery with almost everyone around me. I can only imagine how draining I was to be around – and how often others must have cringed inside when I wore my heart on my sleeve.

What I *wasn't* aware of, though, was the fact that I kept speaking into existence how unhappy I was, *inevitably bringing more of what I didn't want.*

I was totally ignorant that by not taking full and complete responsibility for my own happiness (or lack of it) that I was essentially blocking it, covering it over.

Despite listening to my Father often reminding me of this truth, for some reason, I just couldn't *hear* it. Apparently, I wasn't ready to hear it.

I failed to see that when I pointed the finger outward, I was playing the victim. I couldn't see that when I played the victim I also kept happiness away.

I lacked the real humility needed to be honest with myself and even turned to alcohol for a period of time to temporarily escape the pain that just wouldn't go away, no matter what I did.

I really identified with Pink Floyd's song, "Comfortably Numb" but I was anything *but* comfortable.

If we believe that anyone can "make us feel" anything, we aren't seeing the truth – and we're essentially giving up responsibility for our feelings.

No one can make you feel anything without your consent. In fact, if you look and see, it's almost always what we say to ourselves that determines our experience – and not what the other says.

If you disagree with this then by all means you can be right, but you won't be ultimately happy.

As the fifth youngest of six kids in a pretty close knit family, I always felt that I had to prove myself by trying to one-up you, only to find ways to sabotage myself later, because deep down I felt unworthy.

I was also great at quitting things, including relationships. I'd start something new with great enthusiasm, and then once I got really close to achieving something – that breakthrough moment – I would turn my attention to something else.

I always attributed these things to "well, that's just the way life works." Yeah, it *does* work that way when you're chronically unhappy all the time.

What made it worse was that I'd often hear a voice inside saying, "You're looking in the wrong direction." It wasn't really helpful because I didn't know where to look.

And I certainly didn't know that seeking happiness was an effective way *not* to experience it.

It's like when you're thirsty and you want to cup water in your hands in order to take a drink. What naturally happens if you grasp it tightly?

You won't experience quenching your thirst, will you?

Similarly, if we truly desire something, grasping at it causes it to move further away. On the other hand, when we allow and welcome something, it moves closer.

I've come to love metaphors and paradoxes like this one (life is so full of them) but I love truth even more because its impact is so much more powerful and lasting.

While I see it all so clearly now, I was stuck in a thick and self-induced fog, suffering the consequences of being unaware that I literally created my own experience, moment to moment.

It took many years to see that *all* the unhappiness and suffering that I experienced was meant to unfold exactly as it did … and in fact, could *not* have unfolded in any other way.

Even if a genie granted me the wish to erase those twenty plus years of pain and suffering and replace them with happiness, I'd certainly decline the offer.

The happiness experienced today really *is* sweeter as a result of all those painful years. The happiness experienced today really *is* more delightful because I experienced the opposite of it for so long.

In this world of duality we live in, it's literally impossible to experience true joy and happiness if pain and misery isn't a potential experience, too.

SEE this truth and welcome all of it.

I had a new understanding and appreciation for the true adage that says, "the truth sets you free" … and I wanted more of it.

Once I was willing to really look inside and question everything I believed to be true, things began to improve – slowly but surely.

I saw that for me personally, nothing good ever came from alcohol. I saw clearly that alcohol actually sustained and reinforced that which I *didn't* want.

It was a vicious cycle to say the least.

Thinking that I had intentionally abused alcohol, I naturally felt guilt and shame.

When I finally realized that alcoholism is a disease that induced a physical and mental craving for alcohol, all the guilt and shame that I carried around for so long was lifted.

Seeing the truth, I was set free and yet, I was still responsible.

So when I really saw the role alcohol had in my life and that I'd never be truly happy if I continued to drink – and when I *really* saw that I couldn't be a social drinker (and that I had a disease that made me crave alcohol) a burden so heavy was lifted from me.

I stopped that day (rather it was removed from me that day) and haven't had a drink – or desire to drink in over 12 years.

It was only then that I was able to see the direct relationship between taking full responsibility for absolutely everything in my life (uncaused disease or not) *and* being truly happy.

I soon began to validate this in my experience when I saw that it wasn't possible to be depressed or sad for very long *when I was willing to be responsible for my feelings and emotions.*

Then an interesting thing happened. When I refused to accept responsibility, unhappiness would arise again! As an experiment, I even tried to take partial responsibility to see if THAT worked.

As I suspected, it did not. I was onto something and it gave me a new sense of purpose.

I was committed to discovering the truth of this thing called "responsibility" and how it worked in my life.

I wanted to find out how my life might be different if I actually took responsibility for everything that showed up in my experience, regardless of whether I believed I was the source or not.

So little by little by little, my life began to improve and happiness wasn't so elusive anymore. I started noticing happiness arise for just being alive, for just being able to see, touch, feel, taste and hear.

I saw that I wasn't entitled to enjoy these physical tools of perception that allowed me to intimately experience the beauty and diversity that life continually bestowed – including all the pains, struggles and challenges, too.

I saw that these sensory tools were truly gifts I received in order for me to experience and express myself in this life – and not something I earned or had rights to.

I no longer took for granted that I could walk, talk, laugh and cry. Birds singing, squirrels running up and down trees, dogs playing, my adorable ragdoll cat napping and children playing touched me in ways I never felt before.

Every now and then tears would well up in situations where I saw so much beauty in something that would have seemed so mundane before.

And it was all because I saw the truth of responsibility. It was because I saw that being happy *and* taking responsibility went hand it hand.

I realized (in my actual experience) that happiness would always be elusive if I wasn't willing to be entirely responsible for every-thing that arose in my experience.

Whenever I pointed the finger and blamed others for anything in my life, I felt crappy. Conversely, whenever I felt crappy, I wasn't taking responsibility. I couldn't escape!!

Being ignorant to what was really true was the real culprit. I began to see that when I didn't know what was really true, some degree of angst *had* to arise.

I began to realize that when I saw what was true – and what wasn't, that something very different began to happen in my experience.

I saw (and more importantly, experienced) that when the truth was seen, something let go its hold on me – usually for good.

I finally understood that when I really saw the truth of *anything,* that I was no longer owned by that thing.

Wow.

I came to see that when I lived in alignment with the law of responsibility, I felt happier. It was if I was rewarded for it and to be honest, I know this to be true.

I don't mean to suggest reward in the sense of reward versus punishment, but rather in the sense that you reap what you sow.

There was an accompanying energetic feeling (and experience of myself) when I took responsibility that was much different than when I didn't.

It's very liberating to *see* this. The feedback is almost immediate and very clear.

The very fact of how we observe, evaluate and judge anything literally determines our experience.

If this is true then, isn't it plain to see that when we perceive everything as outside and separate from us, we invite suffering and dis-ease, actually call it forth in our experience?

When we run from anything, when we argue with reality, when we don't want what we already have, are we taking responsibility?

No, we are not.

What must our experience *inevitably* be? We get more of it.

Where must this energy go? Where *can* it go? You got it, nowhere but right where *you* are.

We can't fool the law of our experience. It's so consistent, neutral and predictable.

Are you really starting to see (and feel) how you already know all of this?

I sure hope so.

When this truth is seen (by looking and experimenting without judgment or resistance) we can begin to work with ourselves and not against ourselves. We see that we really do create our experience with our beliefs and our perspective in life.

We become aware that to resist *any* part of it is unintelligent and senseless, for we know we are the sole cause of our experience, every time.

In fact, it's never about what the other does; it's always about how we interpret, how we respond that matters in our experience of ourselves.

We finally see that it REALLY IS an inside game and it always was. We just weren't aware before!

We see that life mirrors us. We understand that there are no causes in the observable world; the observable world is the world of effects, without exception.

As a result of this seeing what's true, we render ourselves power-ful and response-able.

We literally gift ourselves with (response-ability) in the only point of power, this present moment.

Is it ever *not* right now?

Take initiative, be the example and step up and be counted in this world. The truth is, you are no less valuable or worthy than anyone else in this world.

If you believe otherwise, it simply means you believe in your conditioning and the BS of what society attempts to tell you. Remember, society is conditioned just as much as you are and quite possibly, more than you are.

Your family and friends (and your circle of influence) can really benefit from the happiness you'll begin to vibrate.

I refuse to be on my deathbed looking back on my life with regret, "wishing" I took more responsibility for my own happiness, especially since I always suspected that it was no one else's responsibility but mine.

I decided many years ago that I would not be in a position where one day I'd look back on my life regretting that I didn't fully show up by taking responsibility for all of it.

How about you?

How do *you* want to feel as you look back on *your* life?

Chapter 12
Gratitude Is The Doorway To Happiness

If a sense of entitlement and an unwillingness to be responsible closes the door to happiness – and believing the thoughts in our head *without* investigating whether they're true or not *locks* that door – then *what* unlocks and opens that door?

Gratitude that's based in reality – and not fantasy – unlocks and opens that door. What's actually happening in *any* moment IS reality.

It's not possible to experience the lasting happiness we desire without being truly grateful for *everything* in our lives.

We've been taught to believe that the best way to feel grateful (*and happy, by the way*) is by *cultivating gratitude* or by creating a gratitude notebook or journal, writing down everything we can think of – that when we *really* think about it – we're grateful for.

If you've tried this method (like I have) you may have seen that the purpose of consciously doing these exercises on a regular basis is to remind yourself of all the things you're grateful for, *should be* grateful for and *could be* grateful for – and heck, let's add – are willing to be grateful for.

While there's definitely some use and benefit to this approach, there's *so much more* to the formula of being truly grateful.

Have you noticed that your actual and direct experience of this popular approach is usually very short-lived, having a beginning, middle and an end ... like all experience?

In other words, the gratitude you feel (as a result of this approach) is a fleeting experience and not something that is organically present most of the time, right?

Like all methods and techniques, it must have a certain life span with a beginning, middle and end. Since this approach is manufactured and created in the mind, it can't last because it's based in that which comes and goes.

Gratitude that's based on conditions and preferences *must be short-lived* because conditions are always changing, always in flux, agreed?

Aren't we usually left wondering why gratitude comes and goes, unlike the way in which the author intended?

And while we have a strong sense that gratitude indeed is the key to happiness, don't we often fail to see *why* it's so challenging to *actually be consistently grateful*?

We may conclude that it's too difficult to be grateful when there's so much "wrong" in our lives. We often believe that if we're grateful for what's wrong in our lives, those wrongs *won't* ever go away, when the exact opposite is the case.

Don't we find it much easier to be grateful AFTER we remove all the problems and suffering from our life?

Isn't our gratitude usually reserved for the people, places and things that we most value and enjoy and not for those we don't value and enjoy?

Because we're wired to avoid pain and gain pleasure, isn't our tendency to be grateful usually conditional? Isn't it easy to meet what we prefer to experience with gratitude – and meet what we don't want to experience with resistance or avoidance?

Isn't this the way most of us have it set up?

As you might imagine, how we meet anything determines our experience.

As in every moment of our lives, we're always at that fork in the road, where we can either resist what is or accept what is – or even be grateful for what is.

It's easy to be grateful when life is flowing in the way we like, isn't it?   However, *meeting whatever arises with unconditional gratitude* swings the door wide open to happiness, but don't take my word for it.

So let's take a different approach, shall we? Let's experiment by taking an approach where we work with ourselves and not against ourselves – because we really do want to be happy.

Can we toss aside (at least for now) the approach of trying to manufacture feelings of gratitude by reminding ourselves of *all that we could, should and might be grateful for,* especially since our intent is for real and long-term happiness?

Gratitude that's not based on circumstance and condition isn't short-lived and fleeting. Because it's based in reality or what is, it hangs around, without our intent for it to hang around.

In my opinion, there's no greater feeling and no greater experience than being genuinely *and* unconditionally grateful for literally everything in my life.

Since I'm aware that in the world of duality we live in, I can't have what I like without the potential of having what I don't like, I'm grateful for both experiences – especially since I desire lasting happiness.

For instance, I'm actually grateful for the fact that I had a problem with alcohol from the ages of 18-34 years old – and for the fact that no matter how much willpower I summoned and no matter what strategy I came up with, I just couldn't consistently drink socially.

I found I could "control it" sometimes, but ultimately I discovered that it was only a matter of time before I was out of control. My experience (and not my mind) told me so.

When I finally admitted to myself that I was in fact powerless, I rendered myself powerful – and something was lifted, namely the obsession and desire to drink.

I came to see that I had a disease that was stronger than my intellect, willpower and intention. I saw that I wasn't in the driver's seat anymore and like a rudderless ship, I was unable to successfully navigate where I wanted to go.

Seeing this truth, shame and guilt vanished almost instantly – and yet I knew that I was still responsible for staying away from that next drink, that is, if I wanted to be happy. I realized that I couldn't have both anymore, so I had to make a choice.

I knew I was not only *responsible for* myself but also *responsible to* those I loved and cared for.

I'm grateful for this disease because it eventually forced me to really look at the role alcohol played in my life – and it led me to doing the inner work that's made all the difference.

There's no closer relative to true happiness than real and unmanufactured gratitude that comes from the heart and not the head.

If you're unhappy in life, you aren't very grateful, either. That's not a judgment, by the way. Just look and see what's real in your experience.

I can't tell you how many times I heard my Dad try to remind me about the importance of "an attitude of gratitude."

He'd often follow that up with telling me how people with a *sense of entitlement* are those that aren't very happy because they feel as if they are owed something.

I'd look at him and nod my head, trying to give the impression that I knew what he meant. Either he thought I was a total moron or he sensed I hadn't truly heard what he was saying because he kept on planting the seeds of this truth for several more years, hoping one day they'd sprout.

My Dad *knew* that it wasn't possible to have a sense of entitlement (towards anything) AND simultaneously have an attitude of gratitude! It's like trying to mix oil and water. It just won't work.

He knew that the two were mutually exclusive. He also knew that to the degree that I had a sense of entitlement towards anything in my life, to THAT degree would I be ungrateful.

Seeing the big picture (and how it all fit together like a puzzle) he knew that to the degree that I was ungrateful, to *that* degree must I experience unhappiness, too.

He'd tell me that an ingrate's frequent focus is on his or her perceived lack and social standing in the community. This insecurity would inevitably lead to a yearning to appear as someone *other* than they were – to "put on airs," as he put it.

This person would invariably love things and use people, leaving them feeling empty and isolated from the world around them.

An ingrate, he'd say, was much more of a whiner than a winner. An ingrate frequently made excuses and blamed others for their lot in life and was generally unwilling to be responsible.

A grateful person on the other hand, is sensitive to themselves and others – and has an abundance of humble, self-confidence that easily praised and supported others.

The grateful person has an orientation of being in service to others and therefore, responsive to the needs of others. And despite any setbacks and challenges in life, the grateful person always has an eye on self-improvement and a better version of himself.

The grateful person isn't necessarily religious but tends to be spiritual.

But most of all, he'd remind me that a truly grateful person possessed integrity (self honesty) and real character built on rock and not sand – and a willingness to do what the unsuccessful people *weren't* willing to do.

I hope he knows – I hope he now sees – that these seeds finally took root and sprouted, with the ability to weather any and all storms that may come my way. I guess the apple really doesn't fall far from the tree.

Thank you for your persistence and non-judgment, Joe. I love you dearly. And Mom, the absolute truth is, is that I can *never* repay *you* for all you've done for me. Never. Raising six kids was the hardest job that required the most love. I love you dearly, Kay.

Gratitude arises spontaneously and is a natural and organic byproduct of seeing what's true. Resentment, on the other hand, arises when we are ignorant of what's true.

For me, perhaps what's most beautiful today is that the gratitude FELT for my parents today isn't created or manufactured out of some sense of obligation or attempt to appear "appropriately respectful or grateful." It's based in truth and therefore, real and lasting.

It's worth mentioning that for many years I had unresolved issues with my parents. I blamed them for a good bit of MY unhappiness when it wasn't their fault. It only kept me stuck in my unhappiness.

I didn't want to see that I was solely responsible for all of it, my perceptions, beliefs, grudges and life experiences.

When I didn't see what was true, I suffered. When I saw what was true, something let go and I was free. My mind didn't tell me this. My actual experience did.

I wasn't ready to see that it was ALL an inside job, always and in all ways. The liberation and freedom I feel today is beyond what my mind could ever imagine. This seeing of what was true freed them, too.

And I know they feel it. Talk about a win-win situation.

It just comes up of its own accord, like the annual flower that sprouts each year because you planted the proper seed, because you saw what was required.

True vision (that leads to true perception) is the catalyst for gratitude to arise on its own, without your intent.

See what's true and the rest takes care of itself, all by itself.

On the flip side, if you don't feel grateful for all that you have or if you've somehow convinced yourself that you're entitled to certain things in life (or anything for that matter) gratitude won't arise much at all.

If this is the case in your experience, then it's a sure sign that there's something you haven't yet seen.

So we see that a sense of entitlement is the *antithesis* of gratitude and that they don't arise together. If one is hanging out at a party, the other won't come. In fact, the other isn't invited.

We clearly see that it's literally NOT POSSIBLE to feel entitled *and* grateful at the same time.

We realize that the best way to feel ungrateful is to feel a sense of entitlement. Feeling *entitled to anything* covers over our natural state of happiness.

Are we actually entitled to anything or is everything TRULY a gift?

If we think we're entitled to anything, we're simply deluding ourselves into believing we deserve that thing because we "earned it" ... or because we're "family" or because we're your "friend"... and that's what friends are for.

If our very life is a gift of grace, then isn't everything we get to express and enjoy in life also a gift – and not something we're entitled to?

Did you decide to be born? Can you take credit for the fact of your very existence? The truth is, it's all grace and it's all a gift, including your life, isn't it?

How would your experience be different if you paid attention to this one truth?

Have you recognized that we frequently feel entitled to those things that we take for granted, particularly those things that are always present?

For example, don't we usually take for granted our next breath, our next heartbeat, the next sight seen or the next sound we hear?

Are we *actually* entitled to our next breath? Are we entitled to our next heartbeat, sight we see or next sound we hear? Are they not gifts also?

Do you suspect that if you were suddenly faced with death that (you'd also suddenly) very much appreciate and be grateful for your next breath? And how about your next heartbeat?

Are we really entitled to experience the wonder and joy and love that this life offers us?

Helen Keller was an American author, political activist and lecturer. She was the first deaf and blind person to earn a Bachelor of Arts degree. This is what she had to say:

"So much has been given to me; I have no time to ponder over that which has been denied."

Do you think Helen Keller, someone who never had the privilege to experience hearing all the various genres of beautiful, soothing music, birds singing, the ocean roaring and babies laughing was unhappy in life?

Do you think Helen Keller, someone who never had the privilege to experience seeing the incredible and vast array of beautiful sights most of us get to see and enjoy, was unhappy in life?

Not a chance.

Not surprisingly, Helen Keller also wrote this:

"When one door of happiness closes, another opens: but often we look so long at the closed door that we do not see the one which has been opened for us."

If there's a direct relationship between taking things for granted and being ungrateful, aren't we wise to see the benefits of being truly grateful for all the gifts freely and unconditionally given to us?

And if what we pay attention to dictates our experience of ourselves, then doesn't it make perfect sense to pay attention to the things we most take for granted, especially since it's happiness we seek?

A thankful heart is a heart that sings a song of joy and peace. A thankful heart can't be an unhappy heart. A thankful heart can't help but look for the good in all situations and all people – and certainly doesn't take anything for granted.

And a thankful heart really does attract the highest good for all concerned because it's inclusive and cooperative.

Meister Eckhart, a German philosopher and mystic of the 13th century said:

"If the only prayer you said in your whole life was, 'thank you,' that would suffice."

Open your heart and be grateful for the countless blessings bestowed on you – blessings and gifts you never earned and were never entitled to ... but only if you want to be happy.

After all, you can never know when your last breath is.

Well, I really hope that you enjoyed this book and I wish you nothing but the best as you continue to uncover your natural state of happiness.

After all, you were born to be happy.

One Final Thought

Remember when you first learned how to drive a car? Remember how you had to consciously think about what to do next, especially if you learned on a stick shift like I did?

After you had a few months under your belt, remember when driving became automatic, where something just "took over" and drove the car without you thinking about it?

This is what can happen for you if you continue to look and see what's really true in your experience. Please don't let fear or any other obstacle (like belief or circumstance) deter you.

Uncovering your natural state of happiness *will happen* if you really want it to happen – and wholeheartedly intend for it to happen. Besides, it's right here and right now, right where you are.

Your own happiness is the greatest service you can render to the world.

Peace and happiness,
Alex P. Keats

www.ingramcontent.com/pod-product-compliance
Lightning Source LLC
Chambersburg PA
CBHW060015050426
42448CB00012B/2771